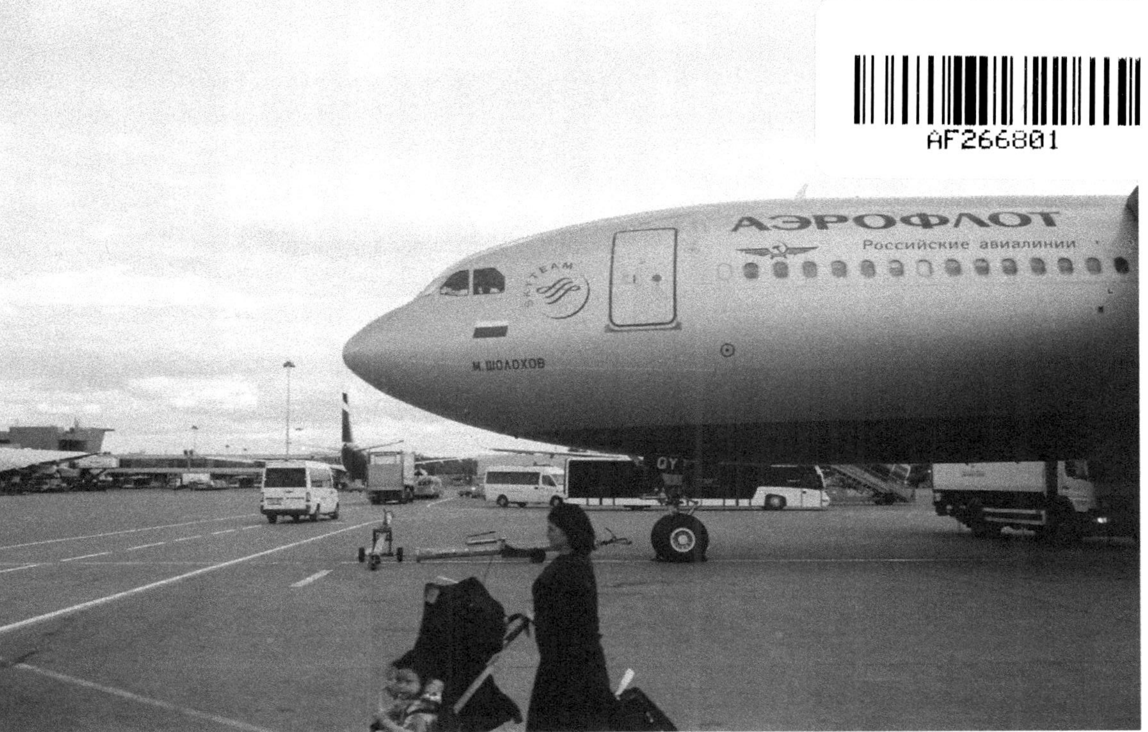

АЭРОФЛОТ
Российские авиалинии
SKYTEAM
М. ШОЛОХОВ

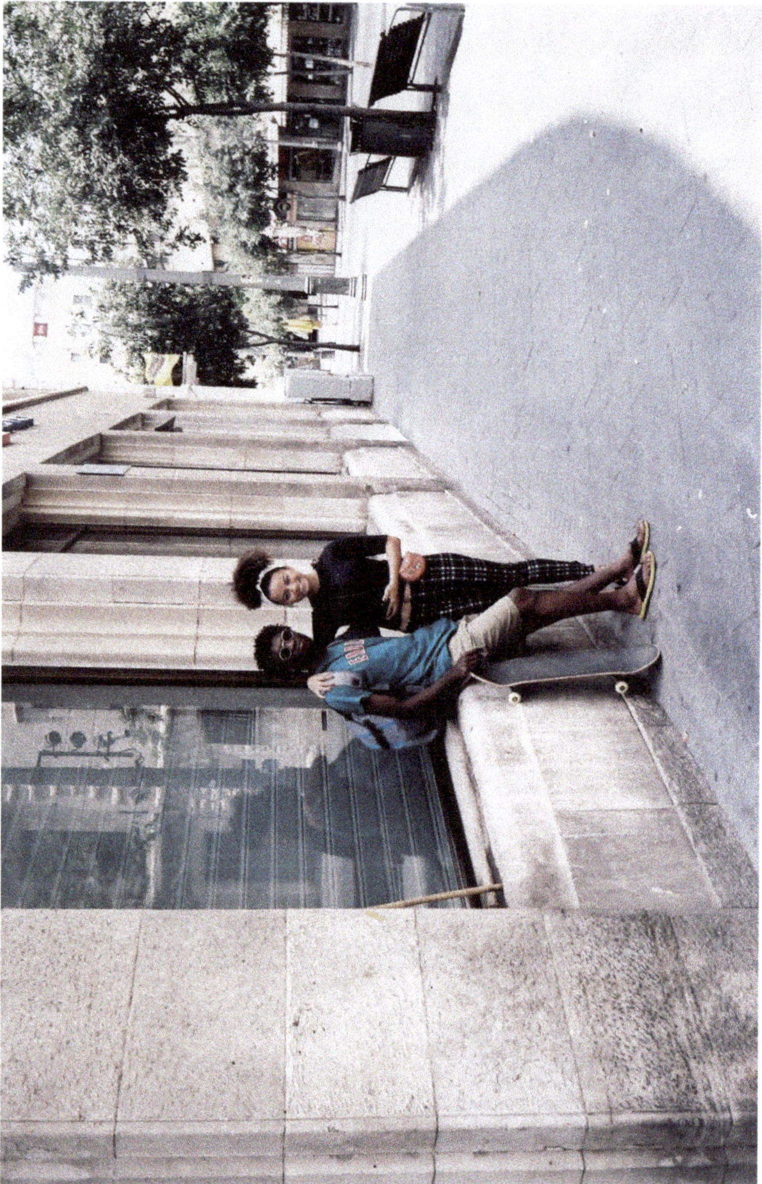

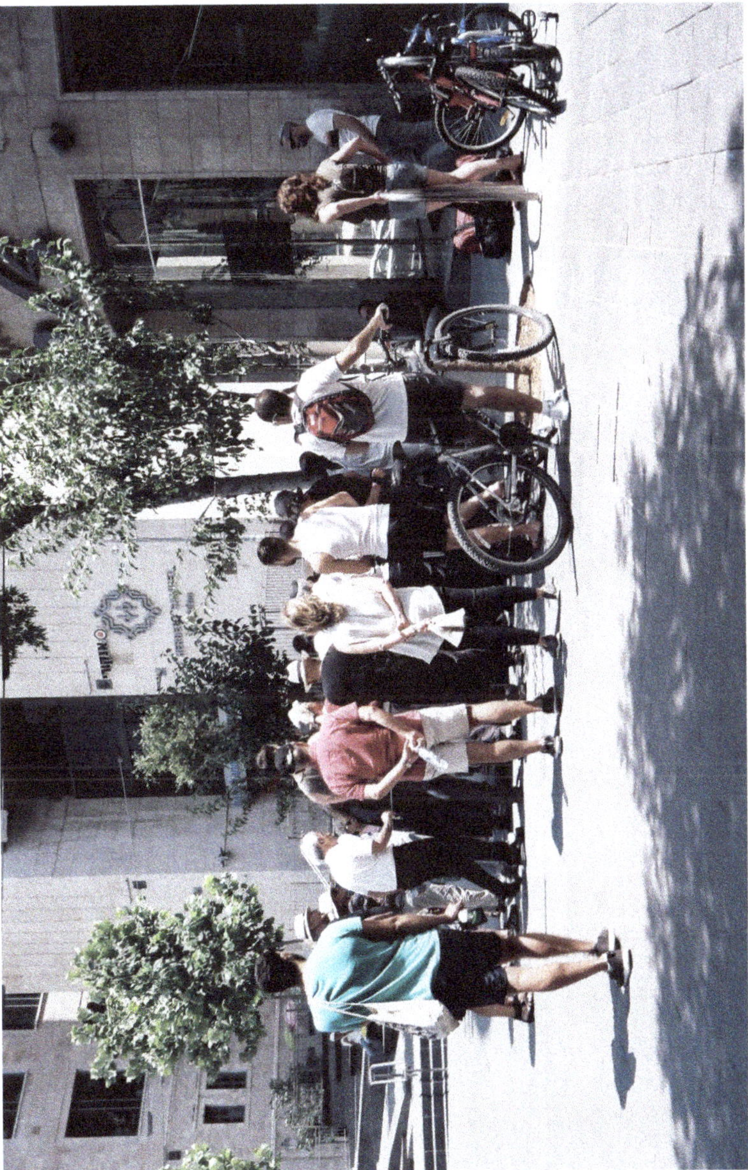

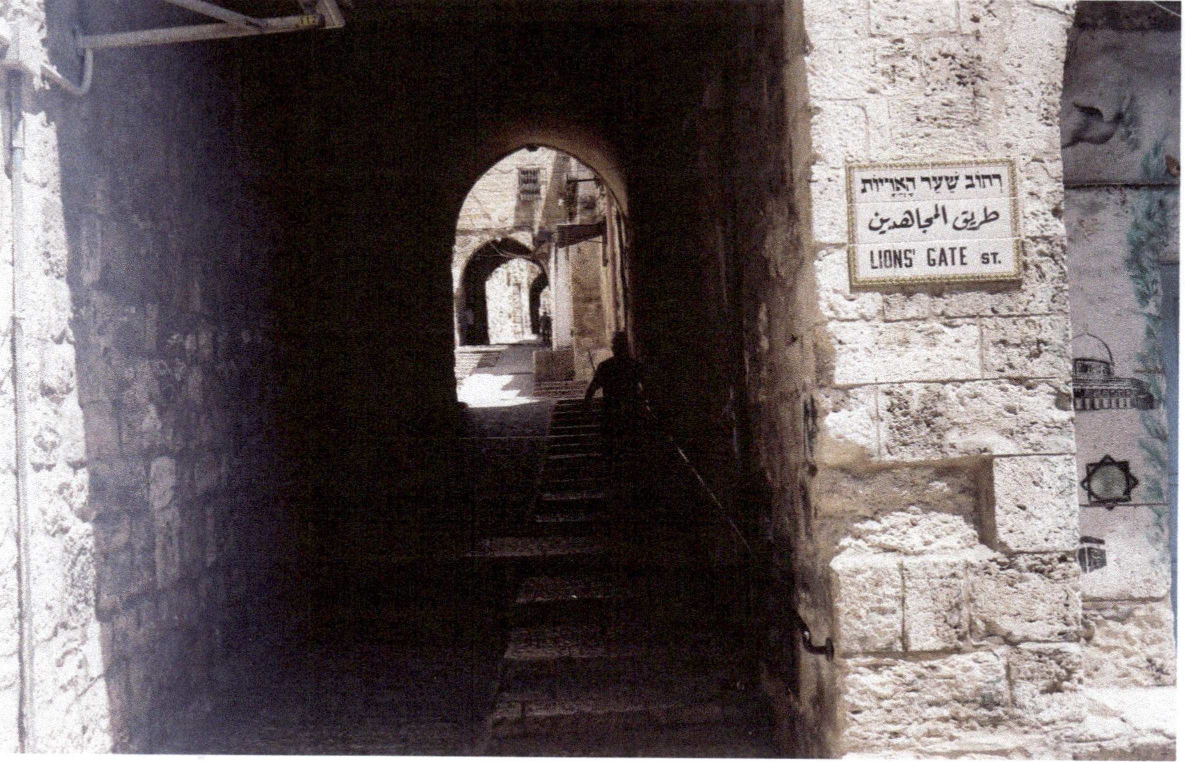
רחוב שער האריות
طريق المجاهدين
LIONS' GATE ST.

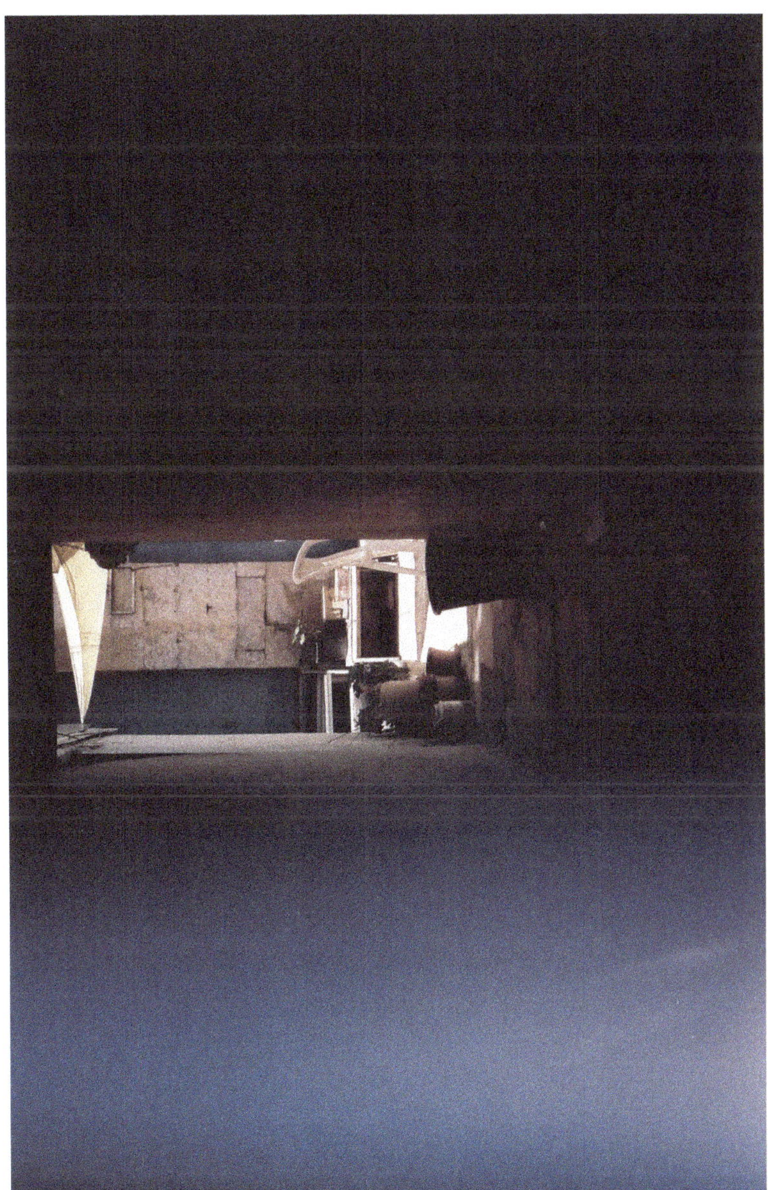

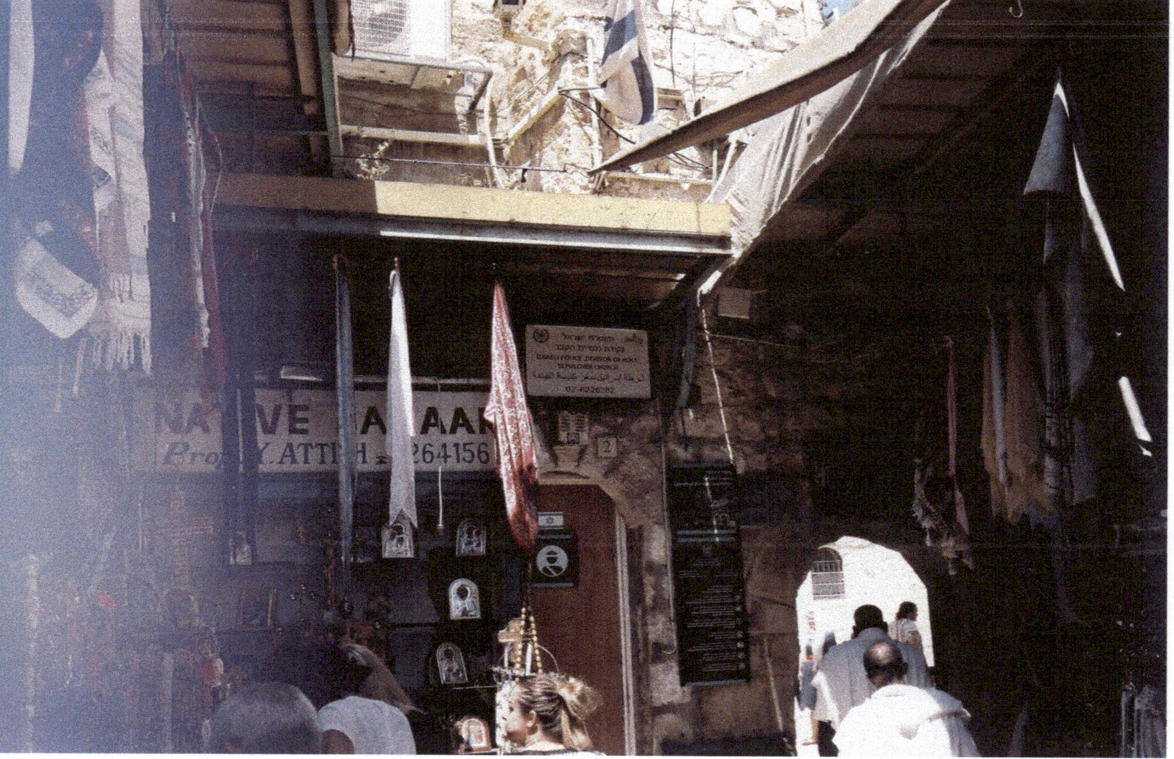
ISRAEL POLICE DIVISION OF HOLY
SEPULCHER CHURCH
02-6226282
NATIVE BAZAAR
Prop. Y. ATTIEH ☎ 264156

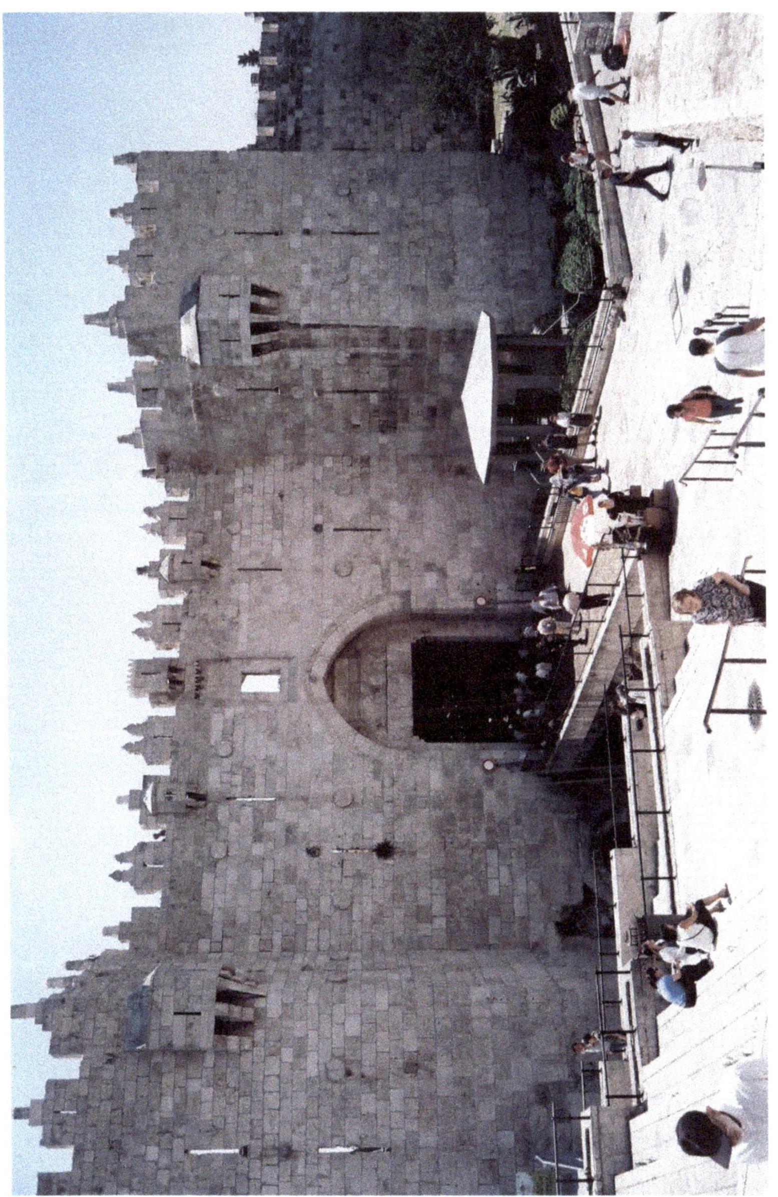

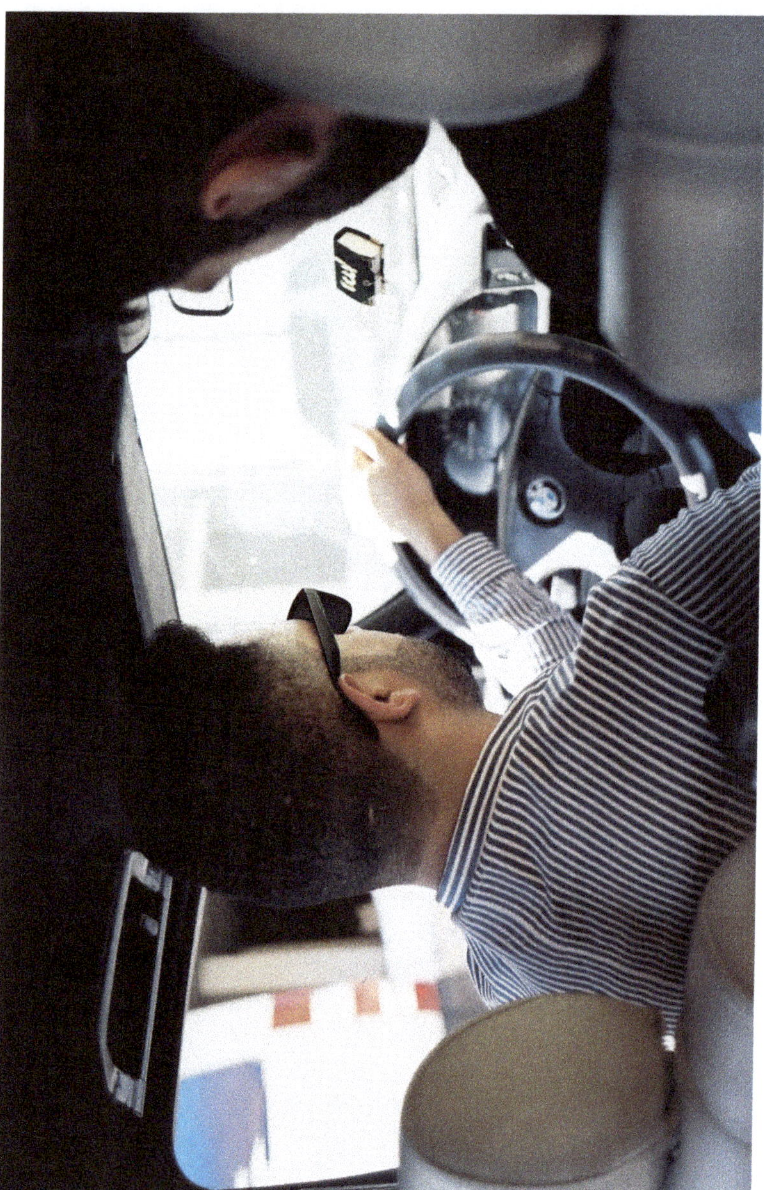

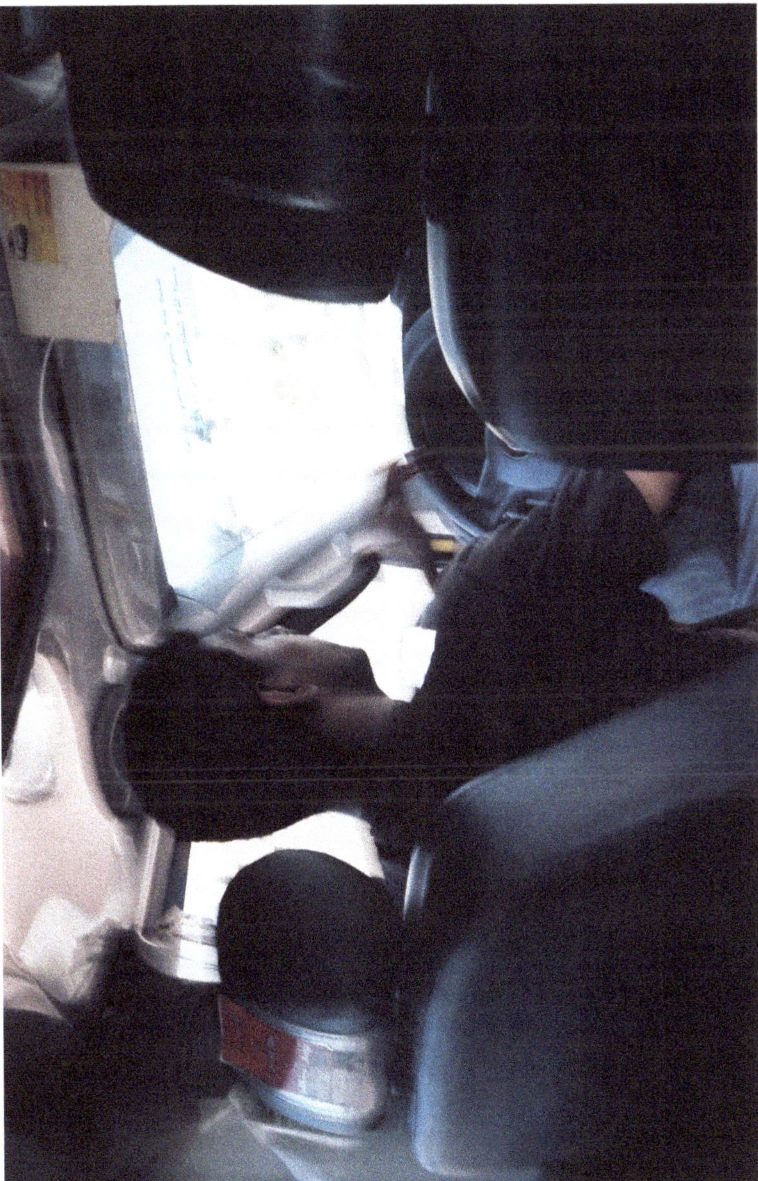

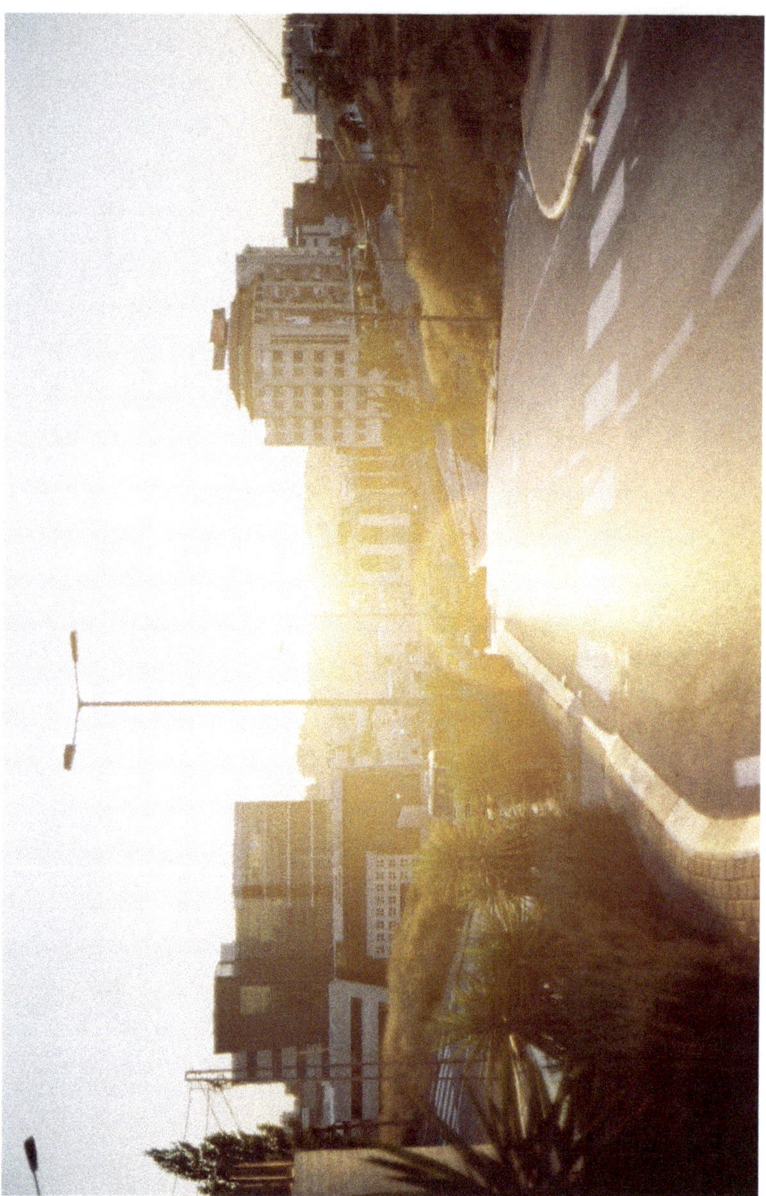

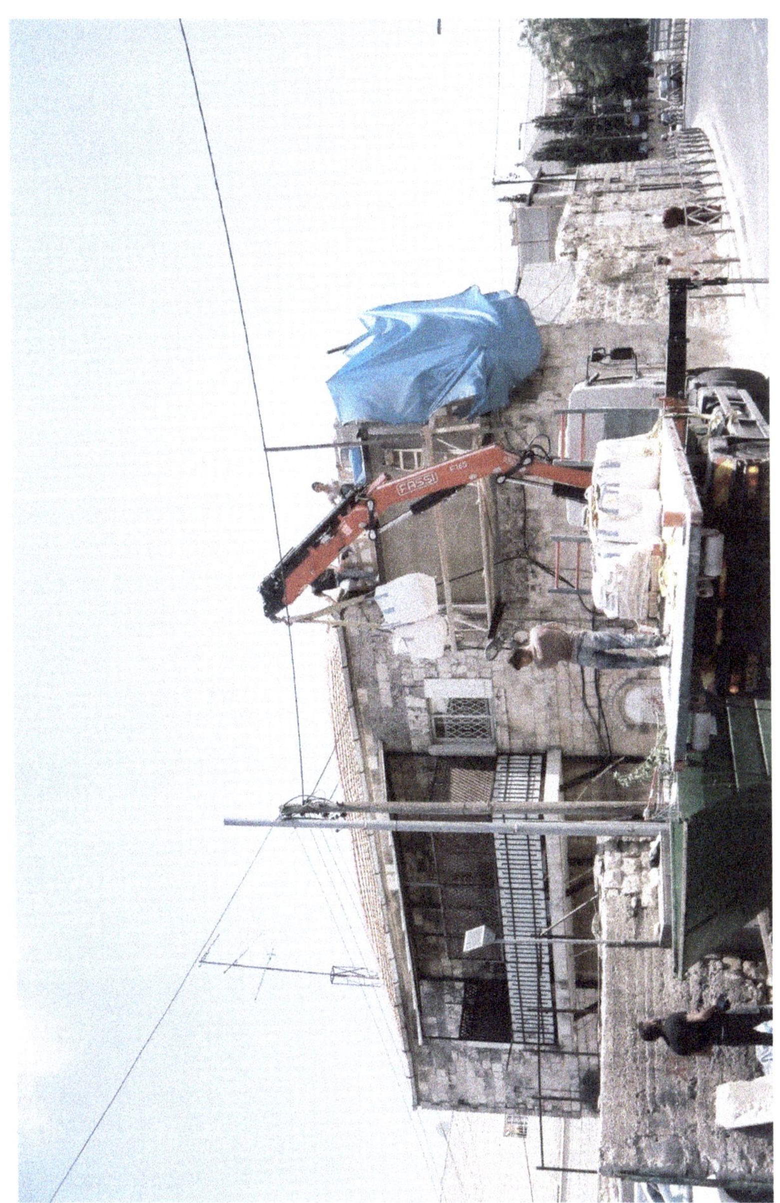

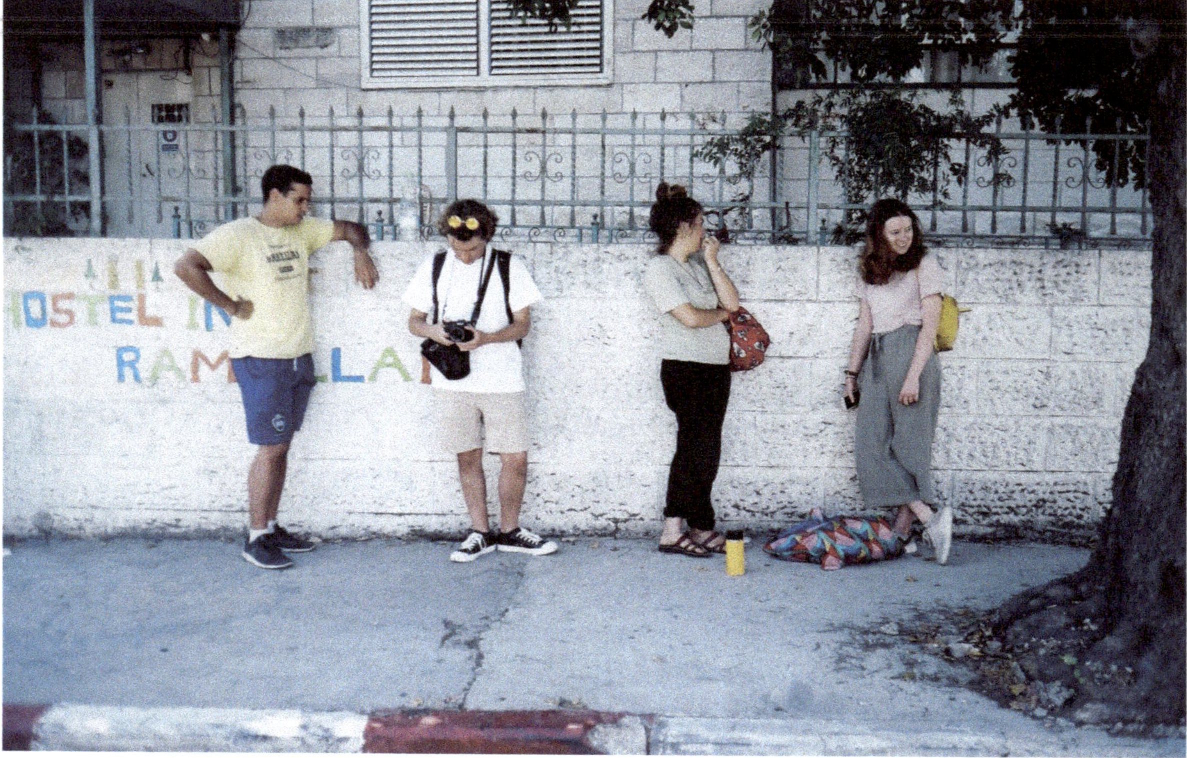
HOSTEL IN
RAMALLAH

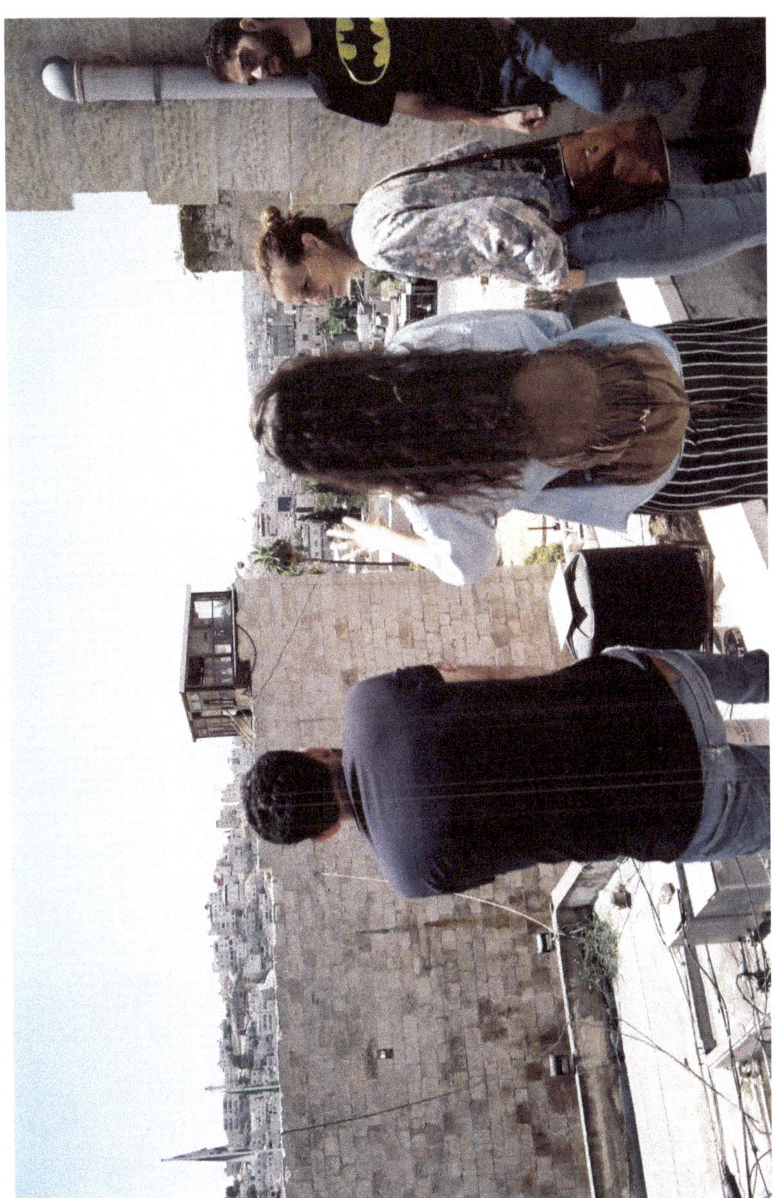

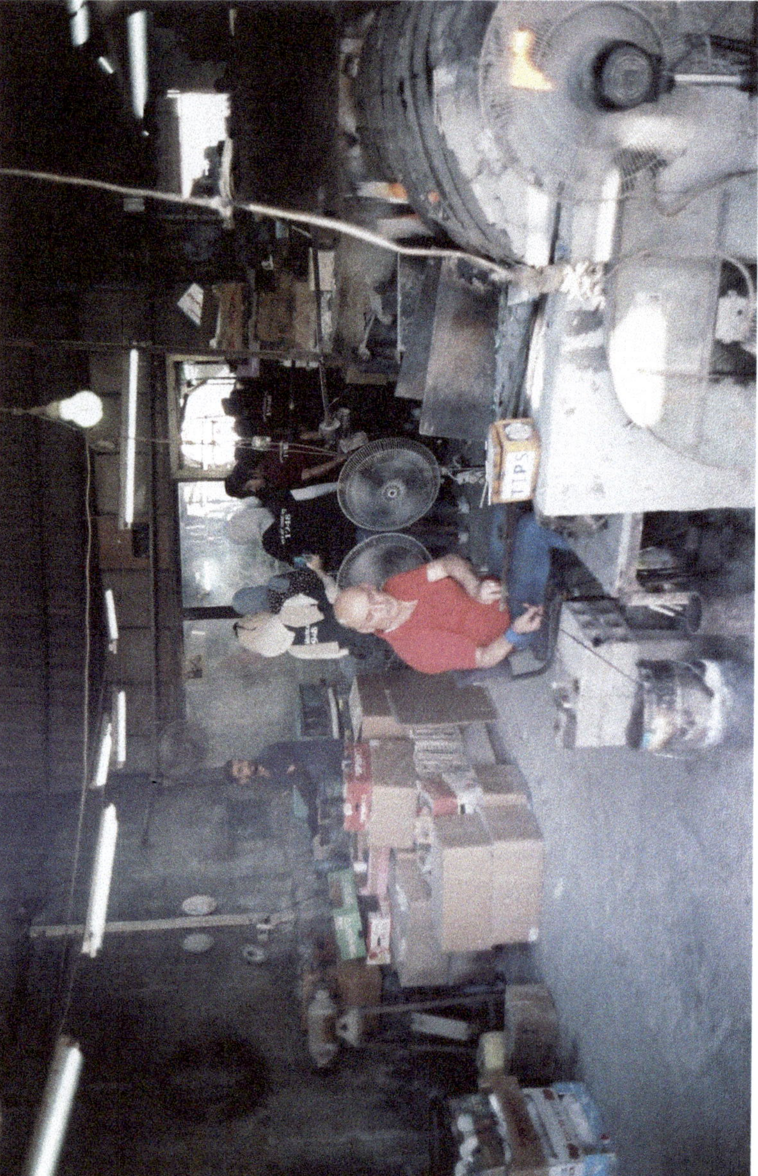

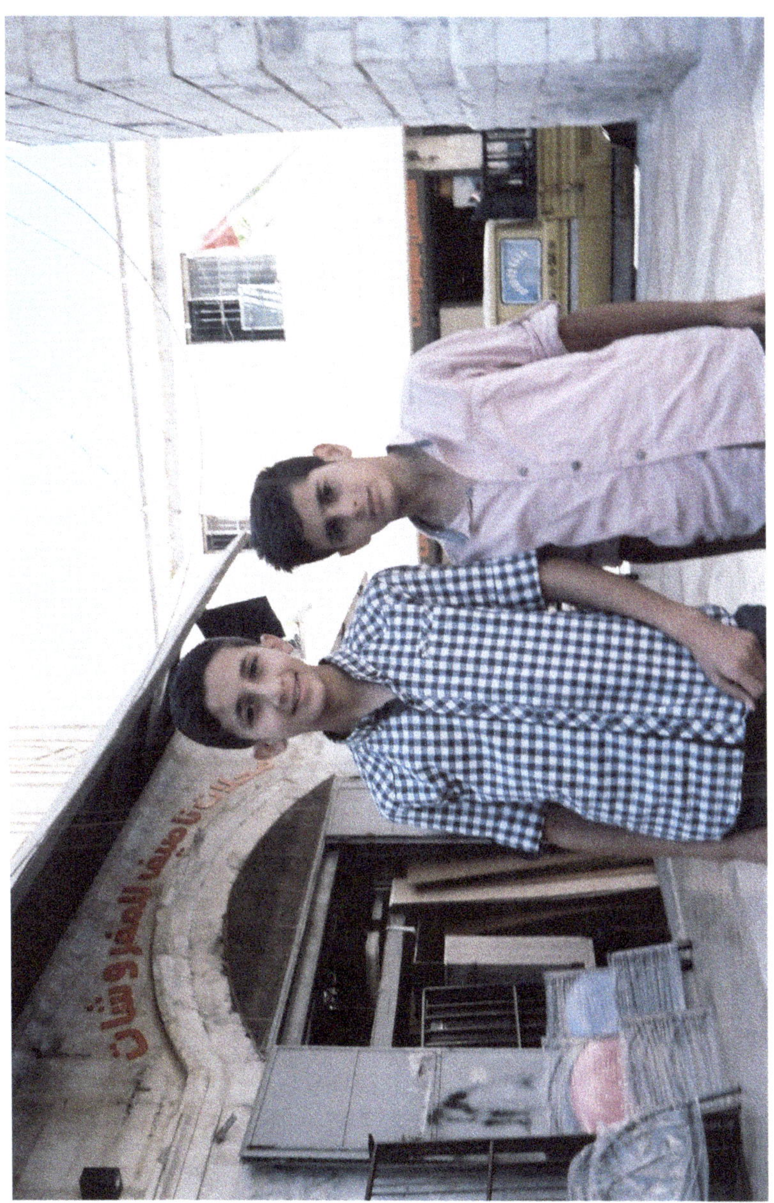

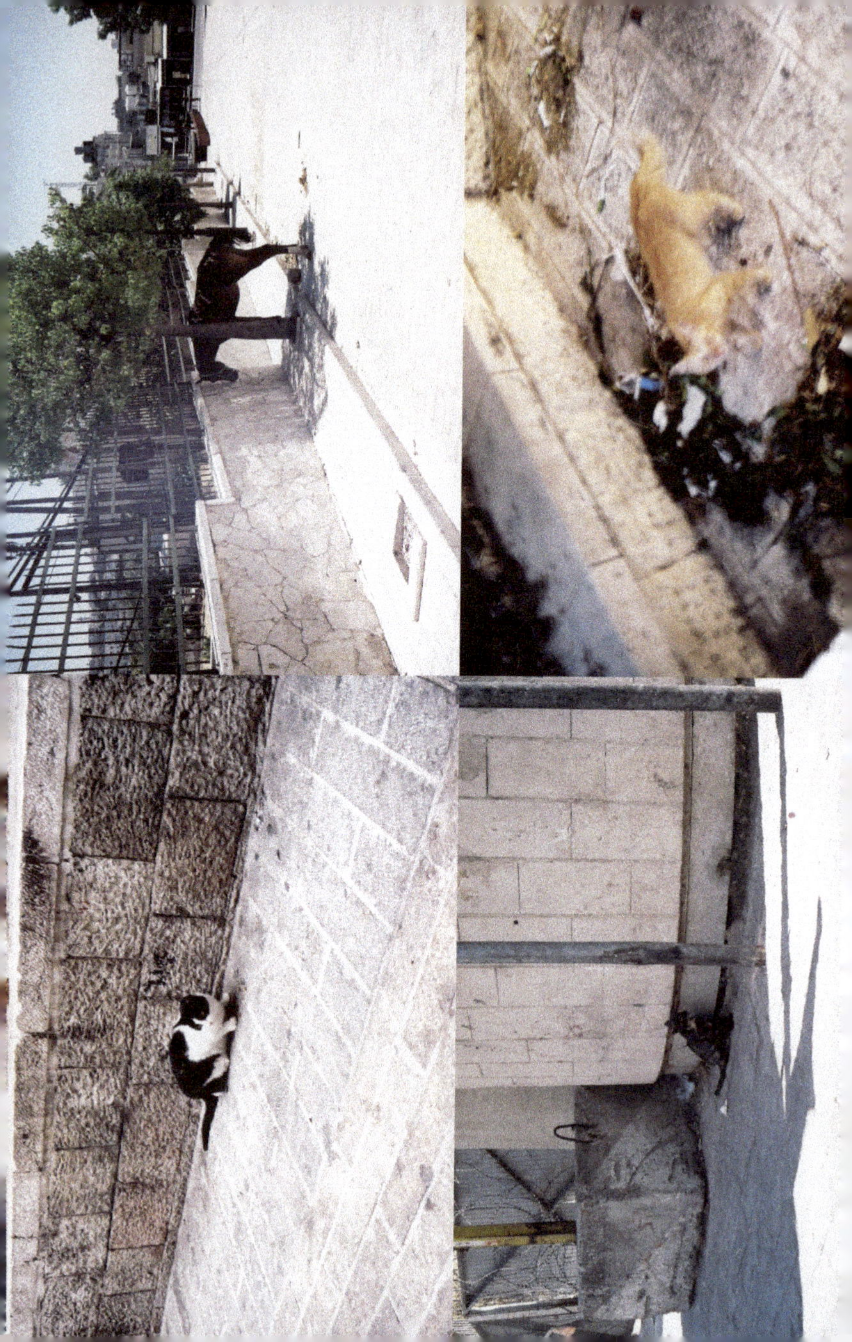

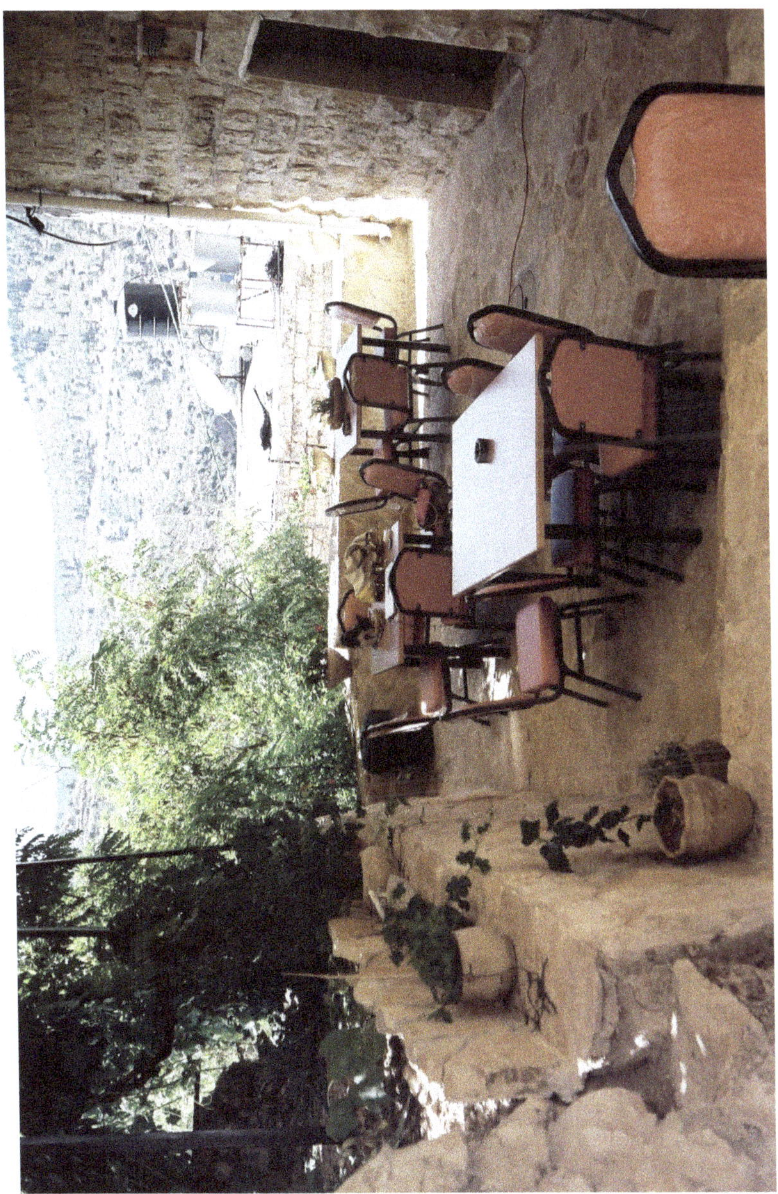

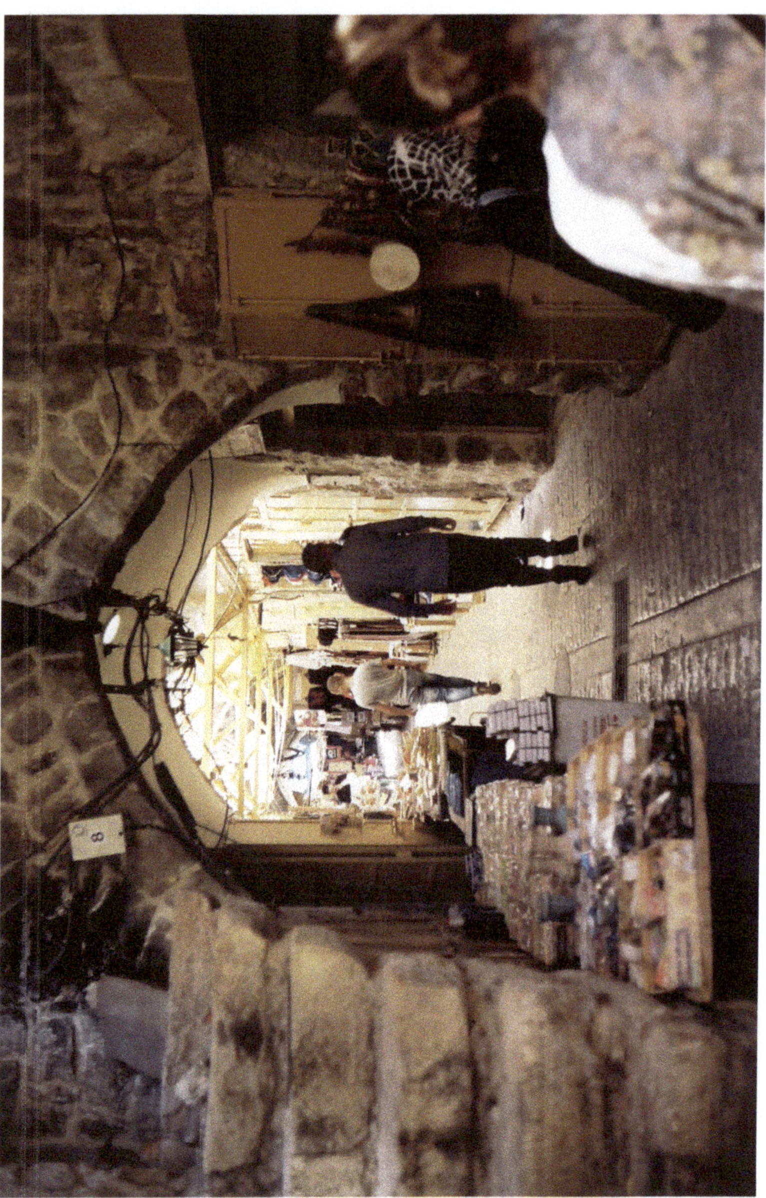

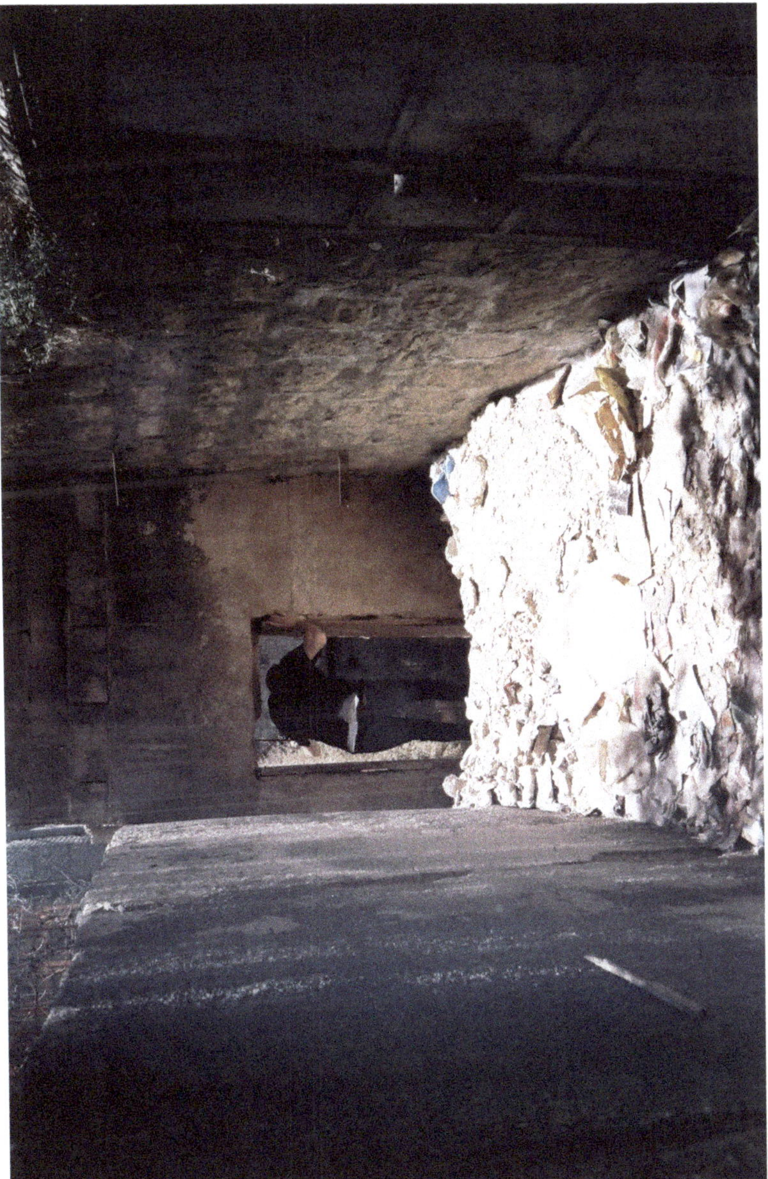

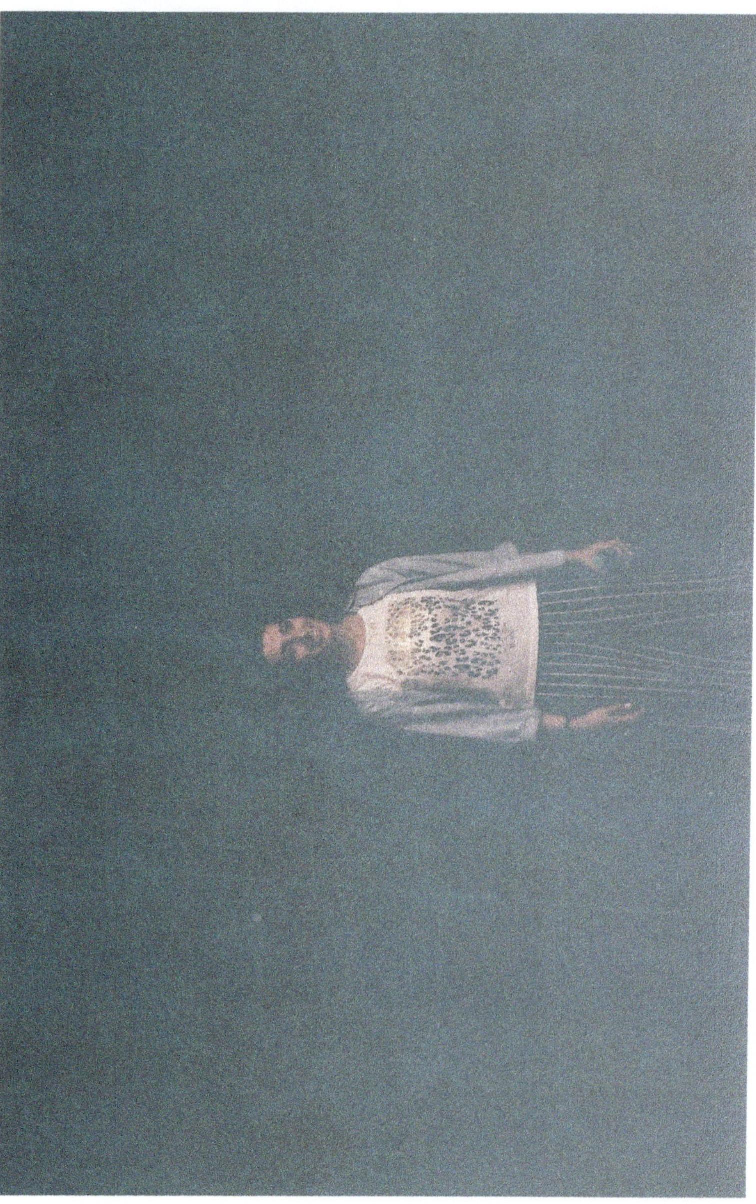

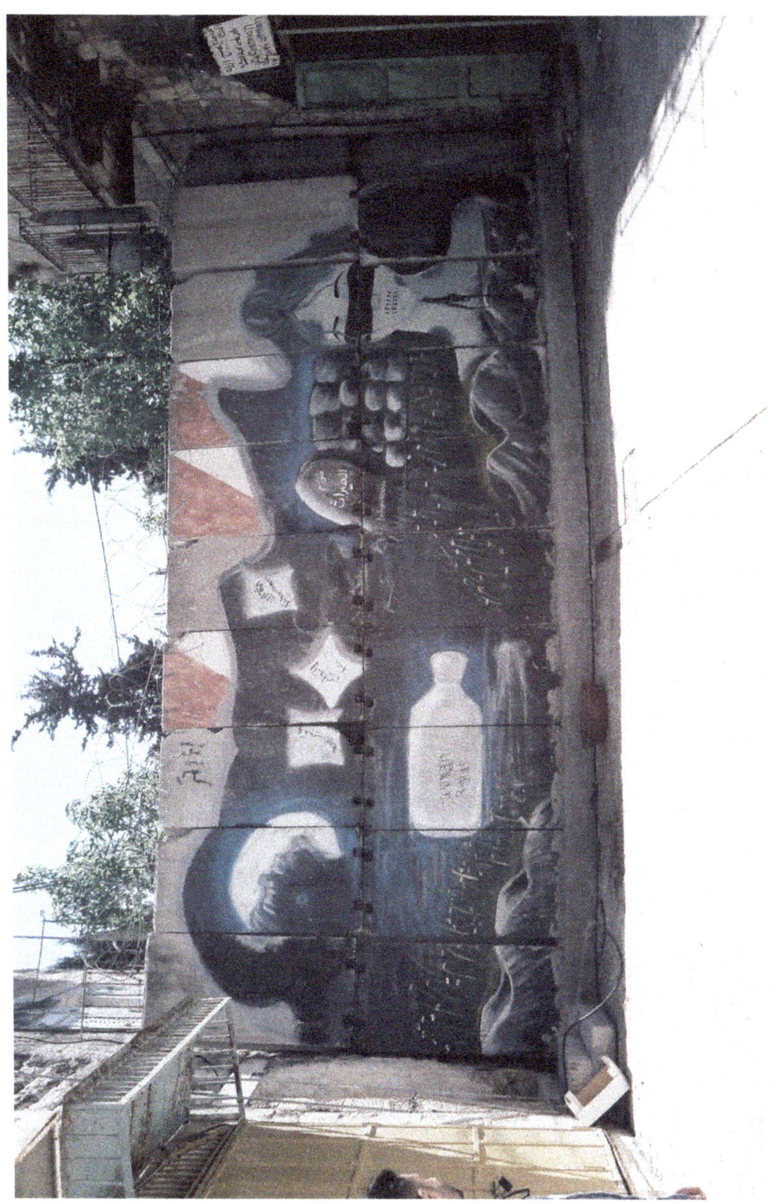

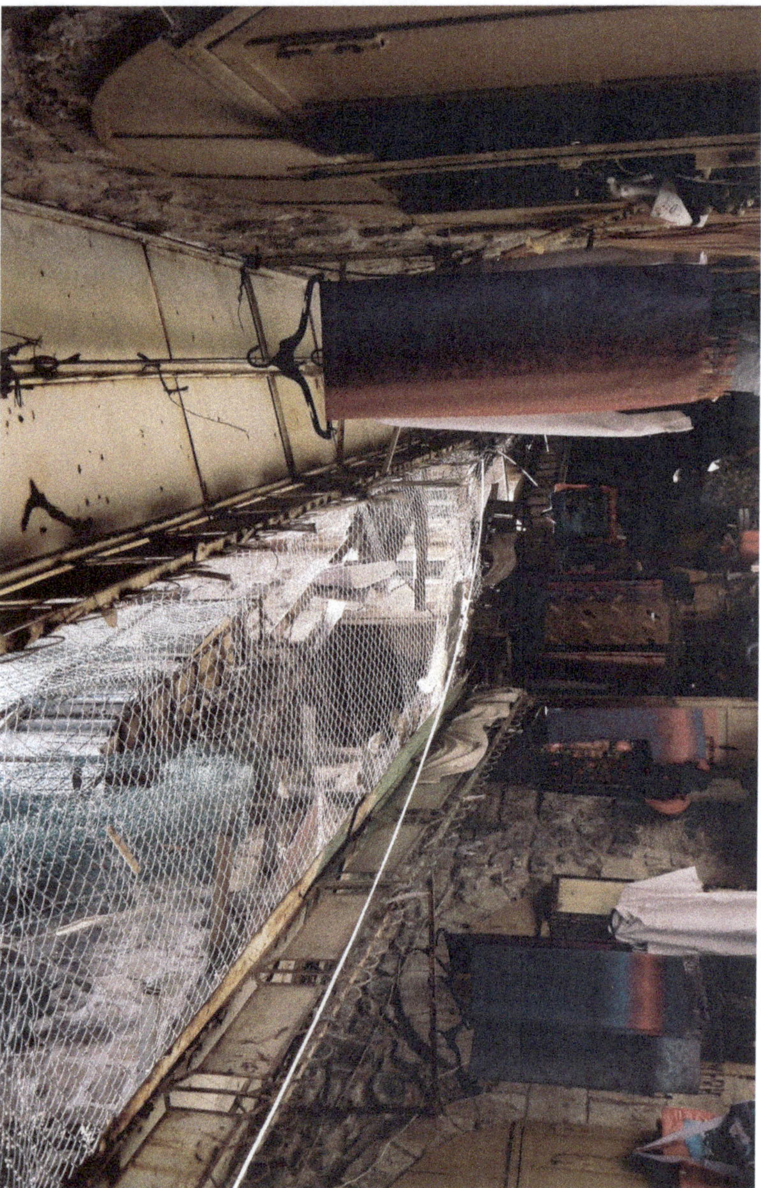

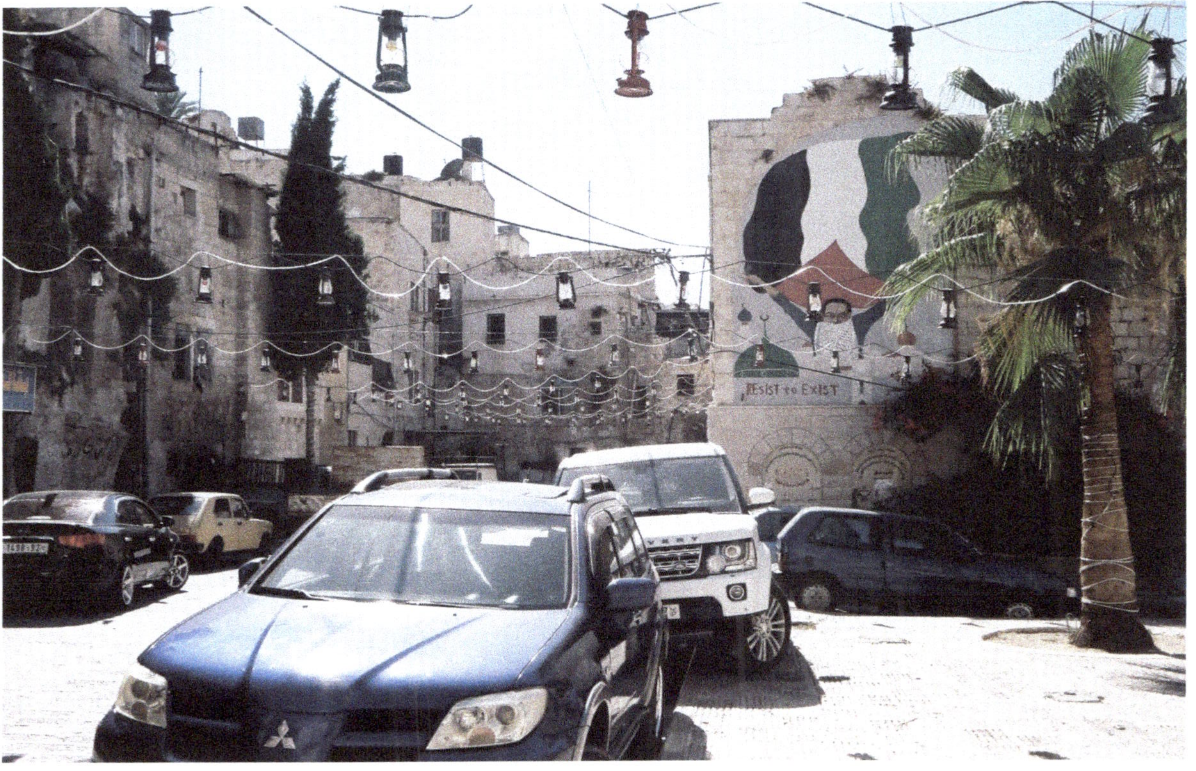

ReSiST to ExiST

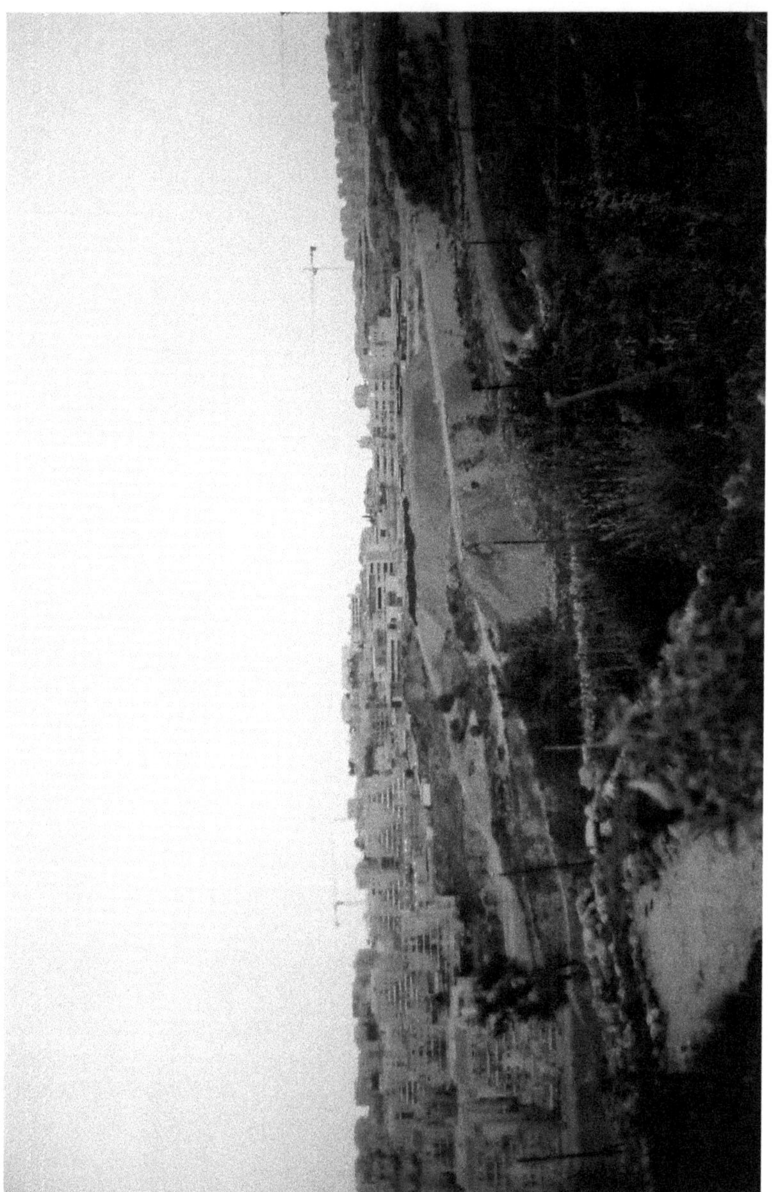

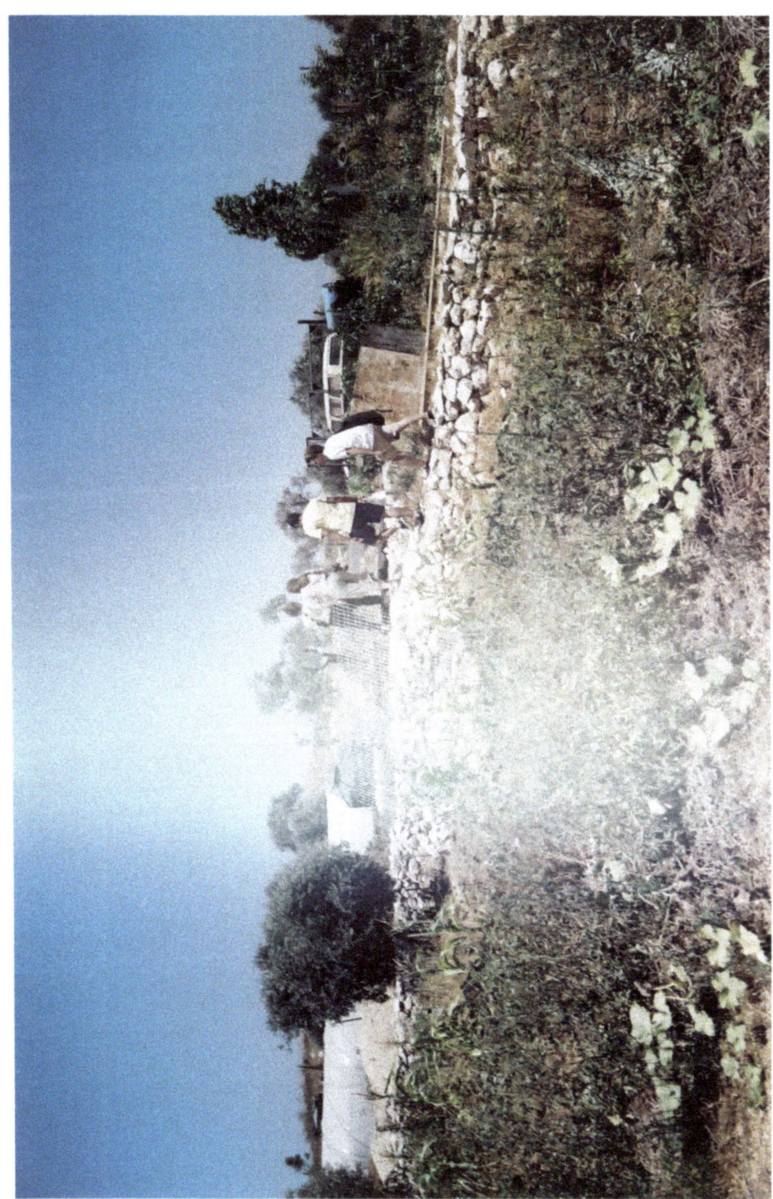

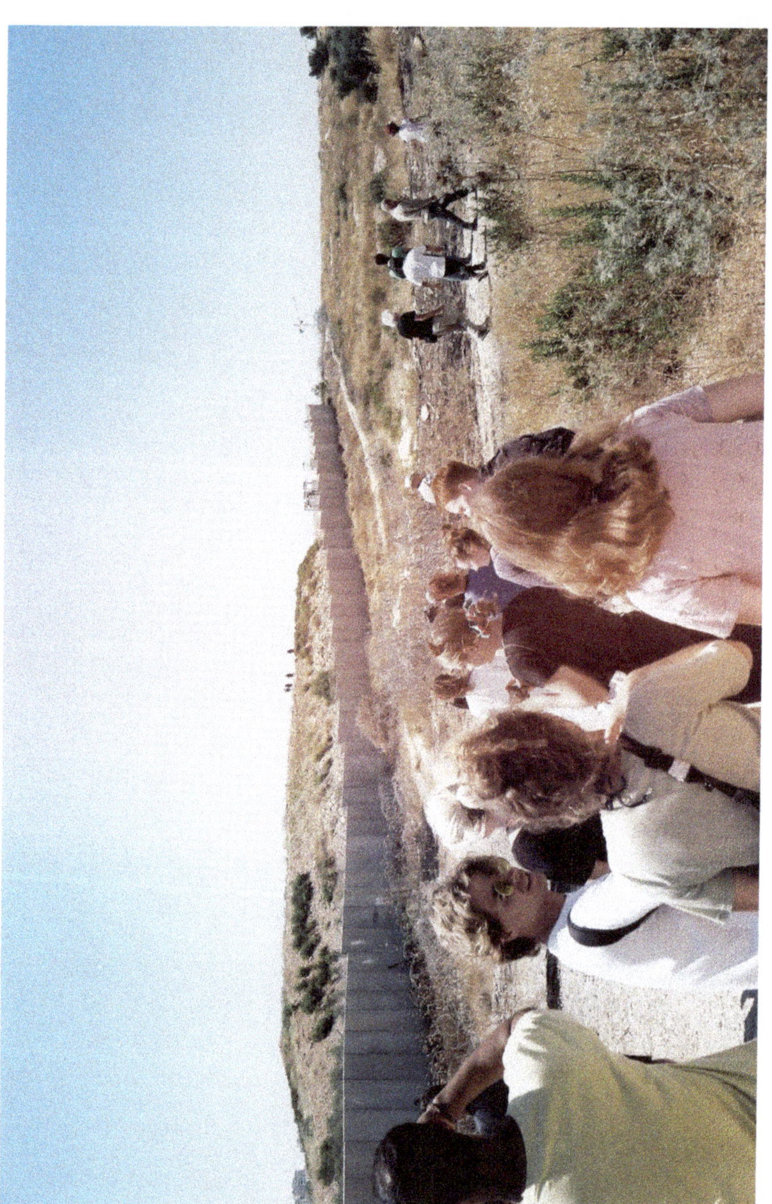

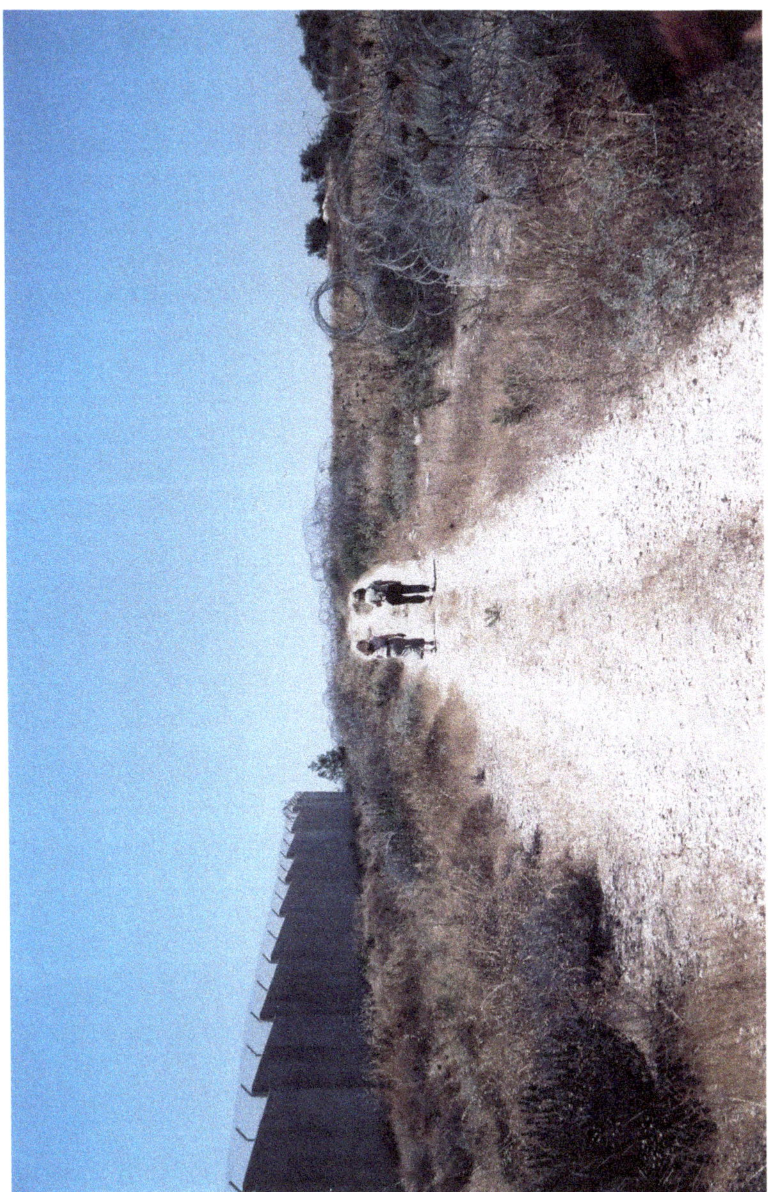

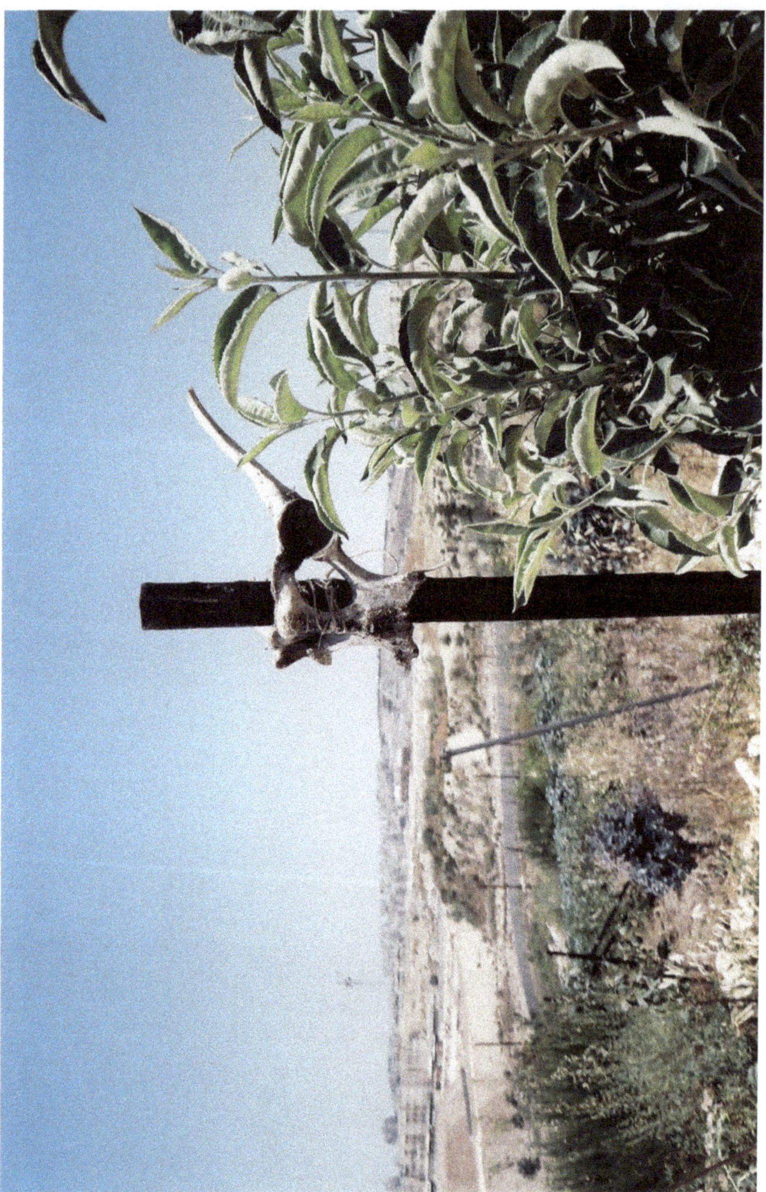

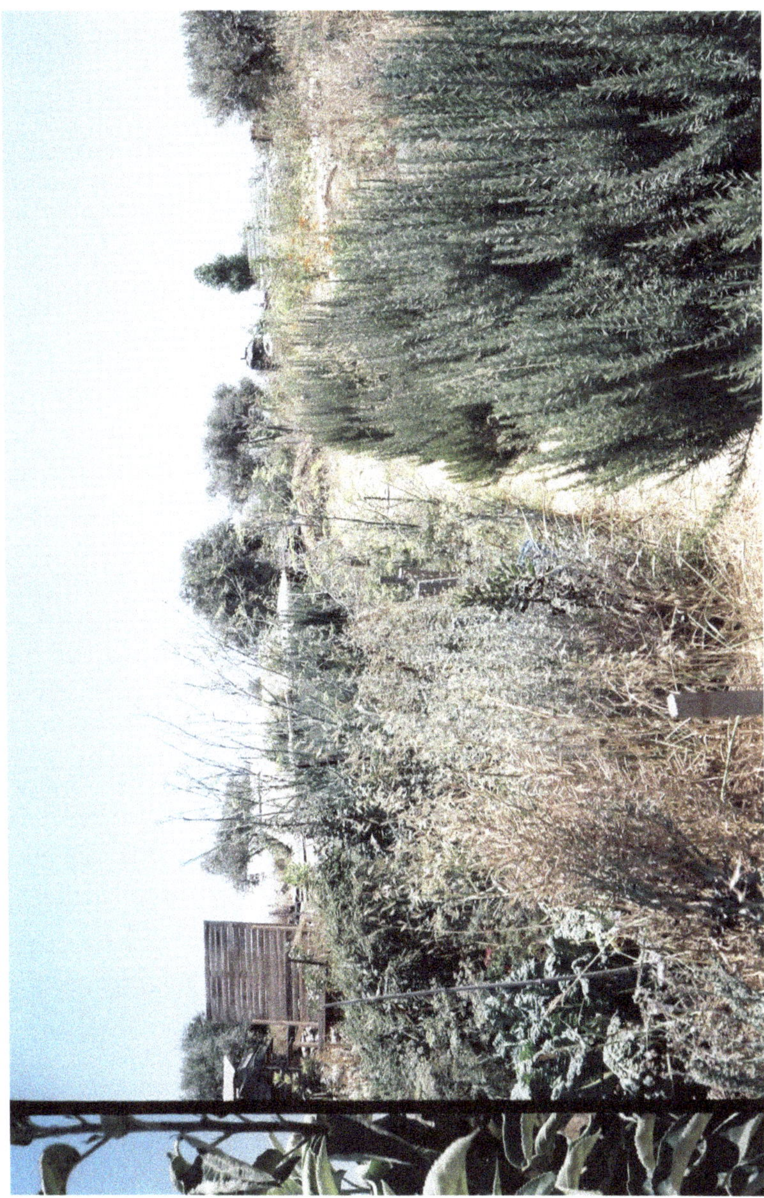

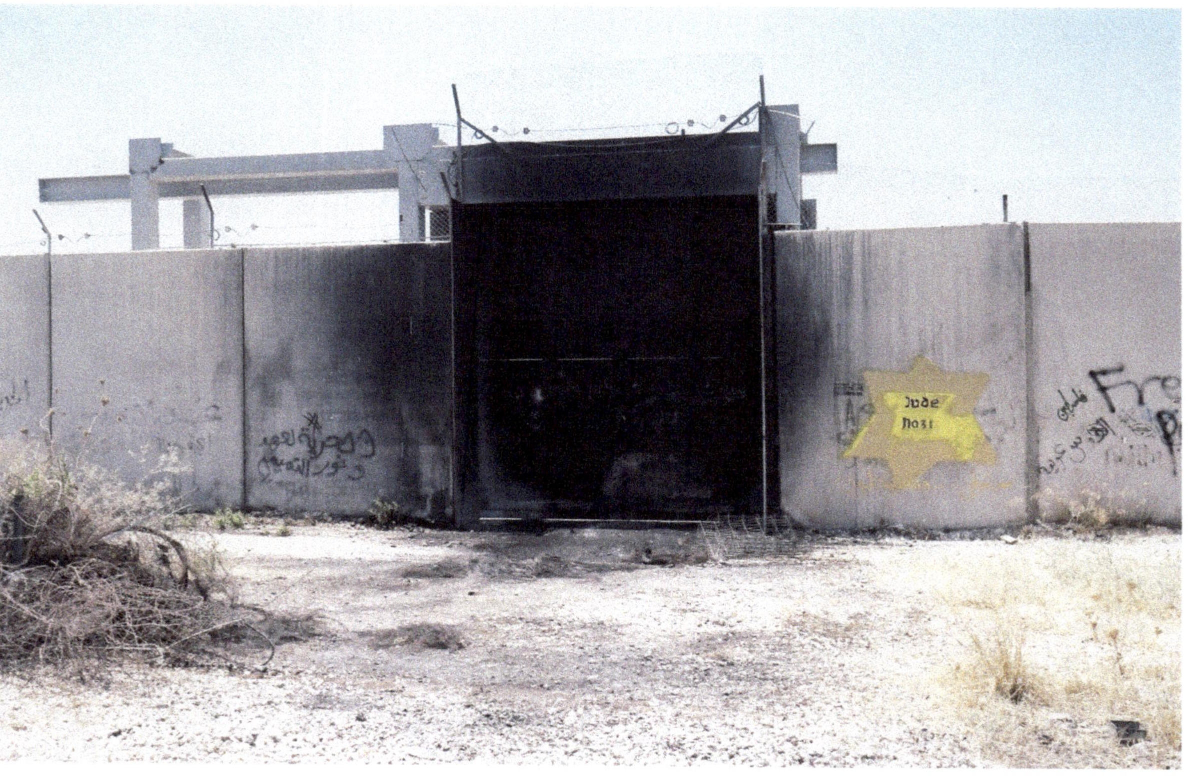

Jude
Nazi
Fre

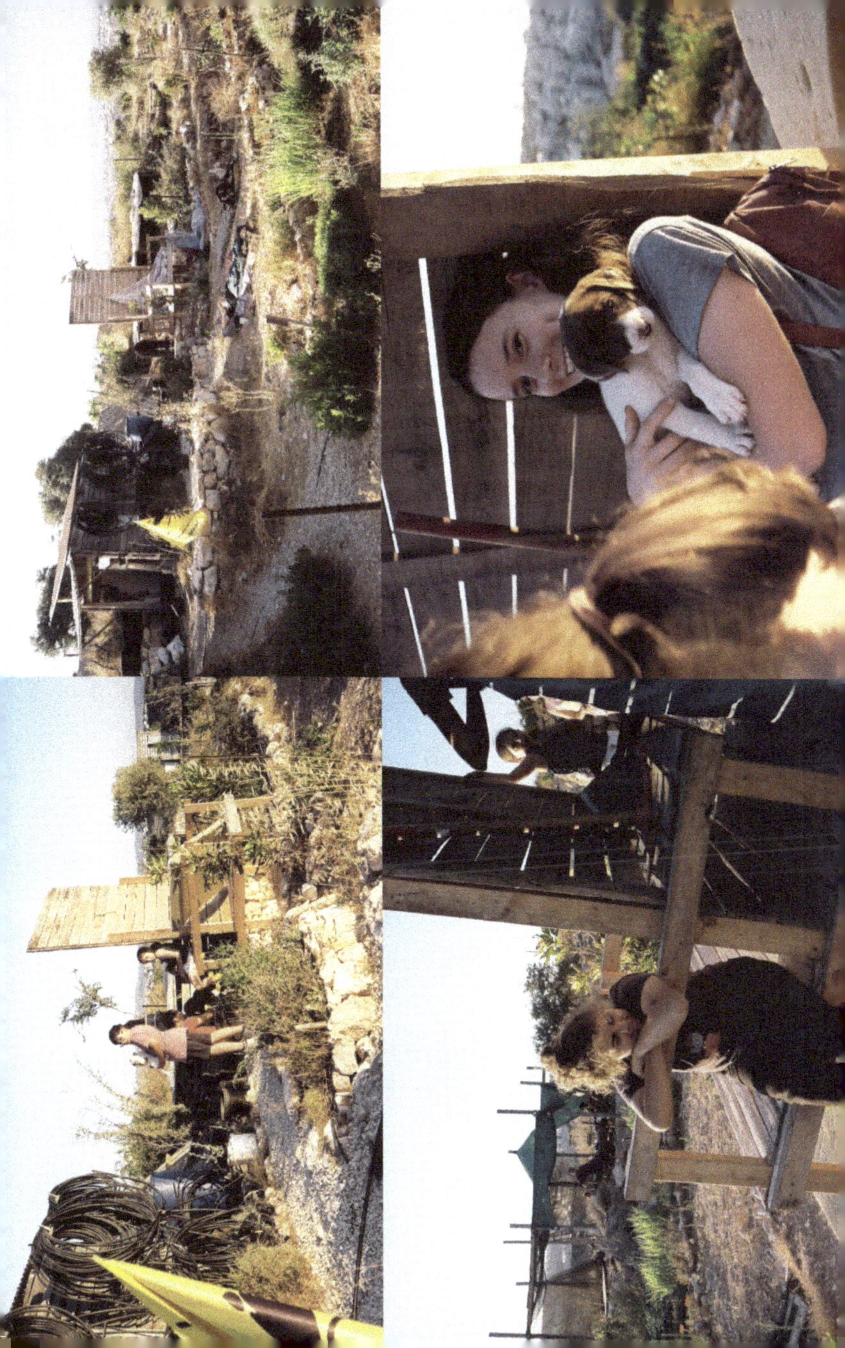

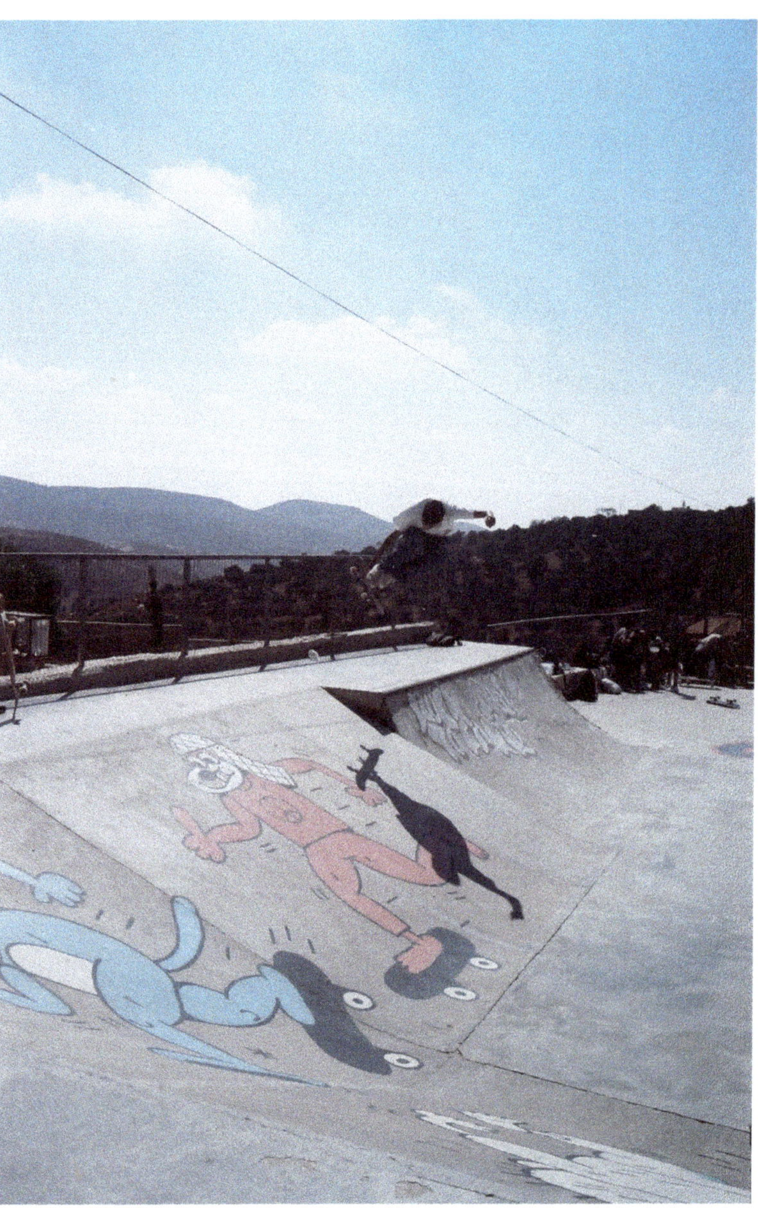

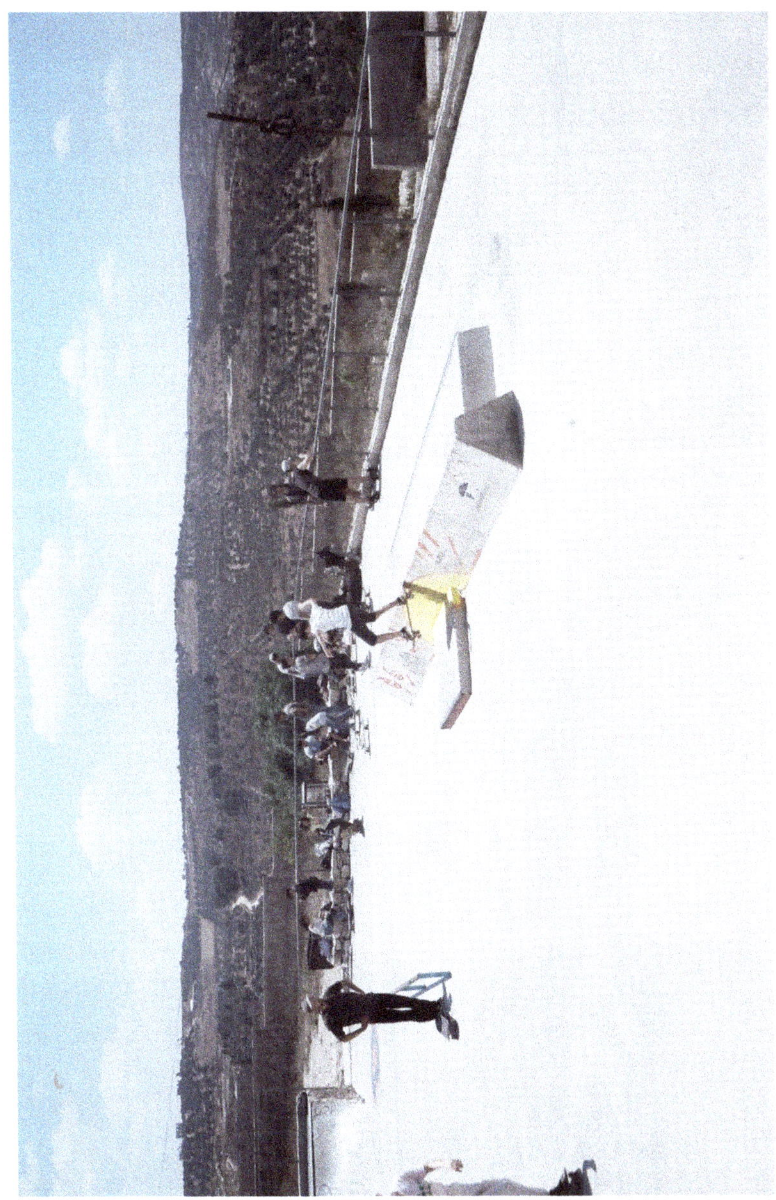

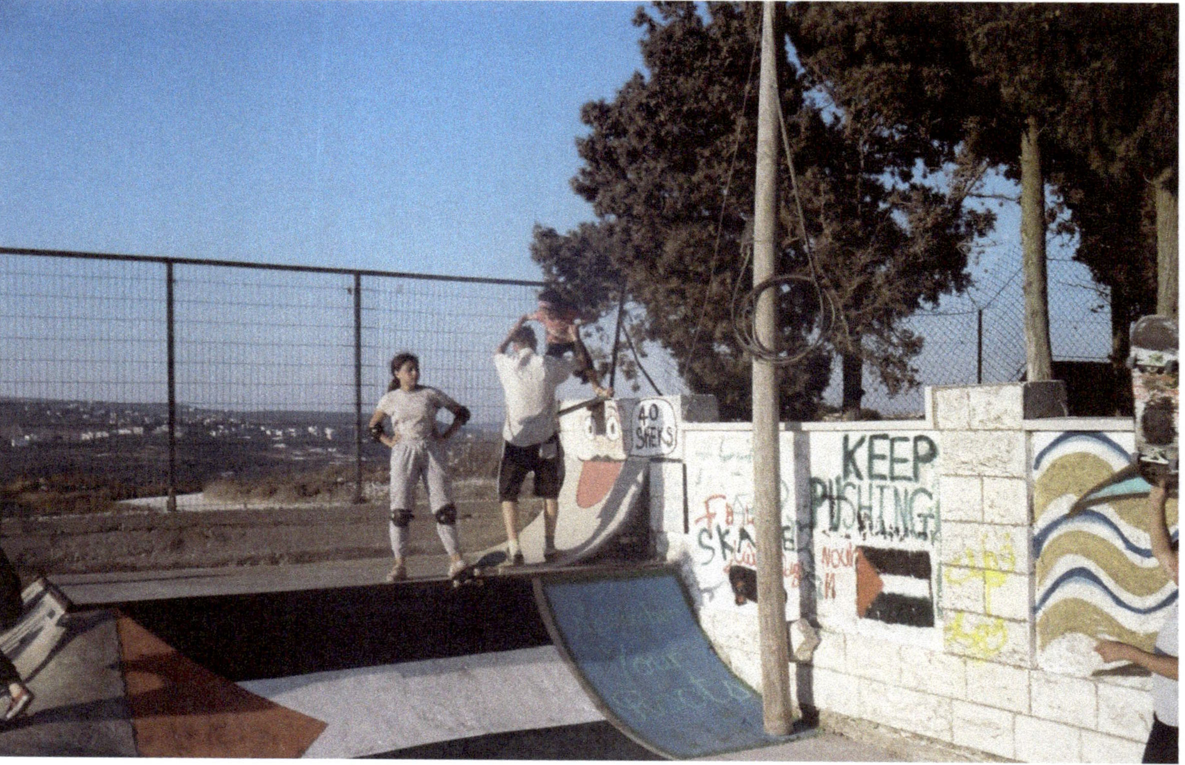
40 SHEKS
KEEP
PUSHING
SKATE

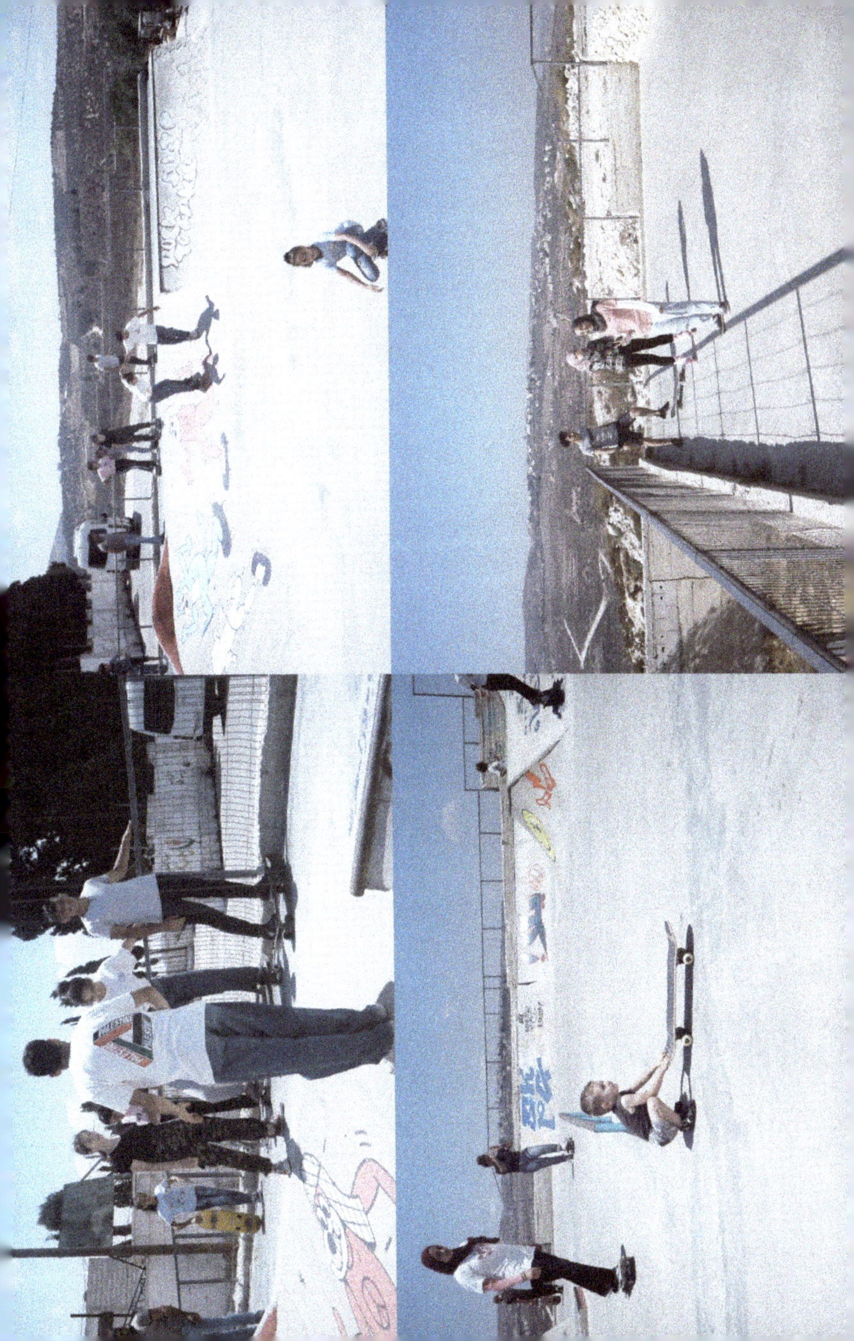

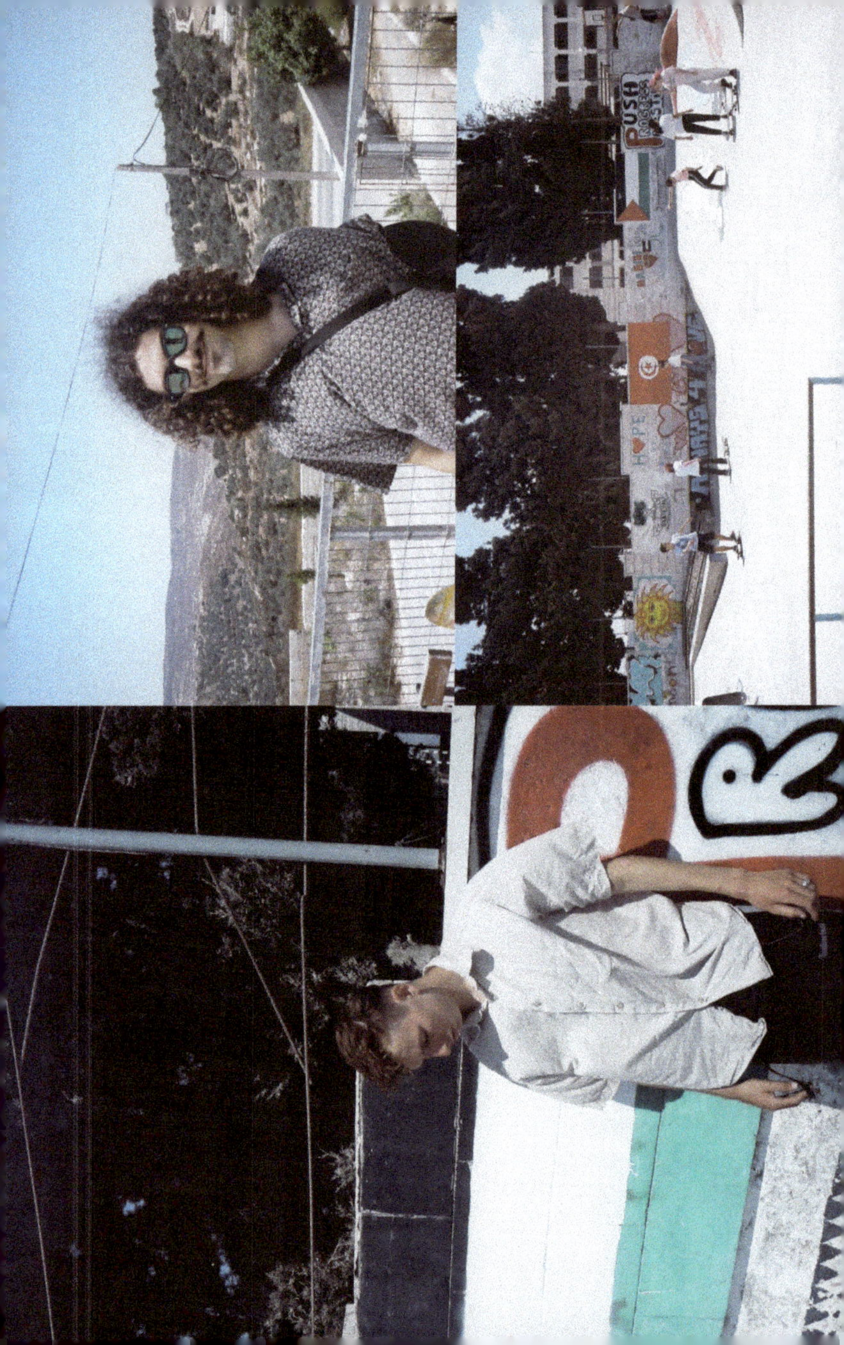

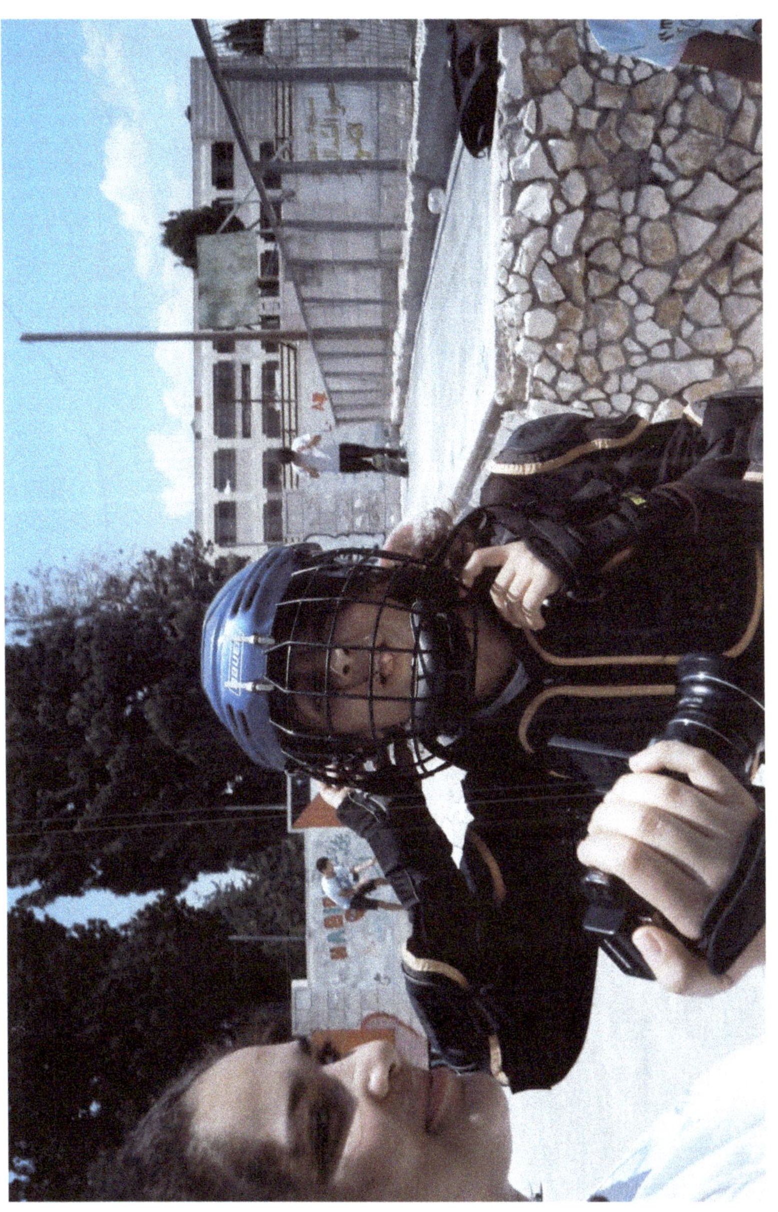

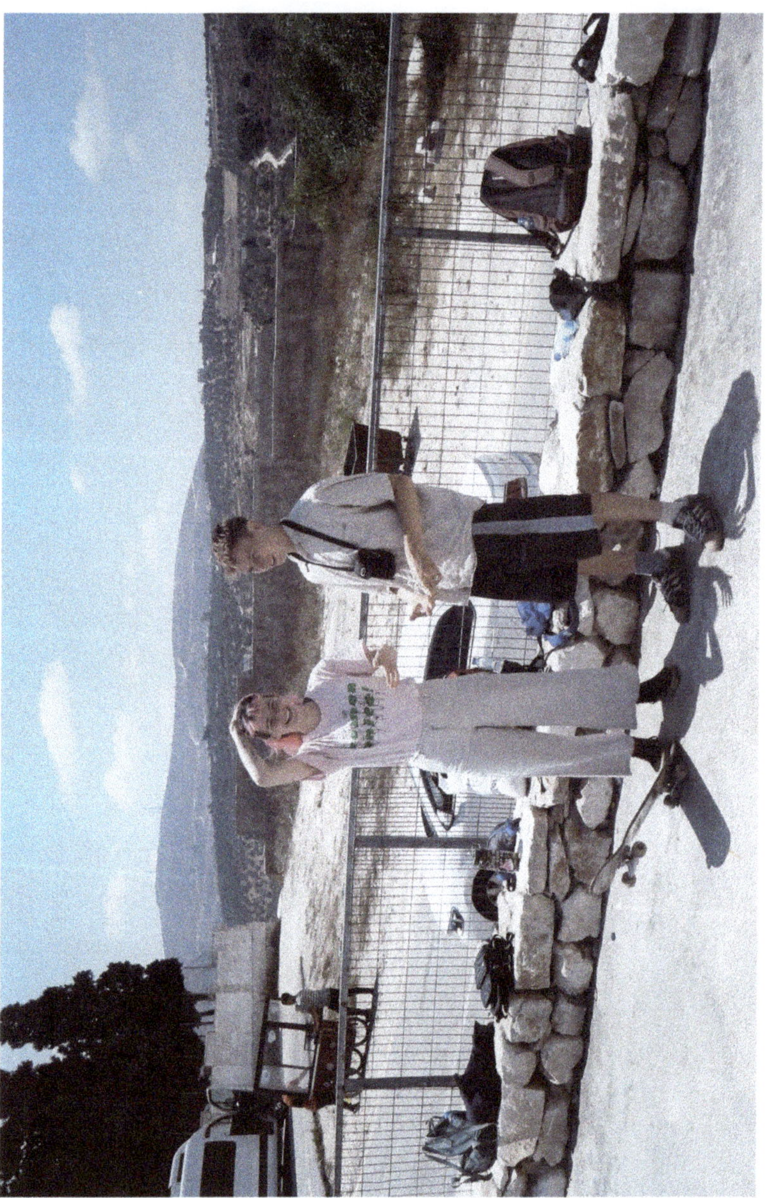

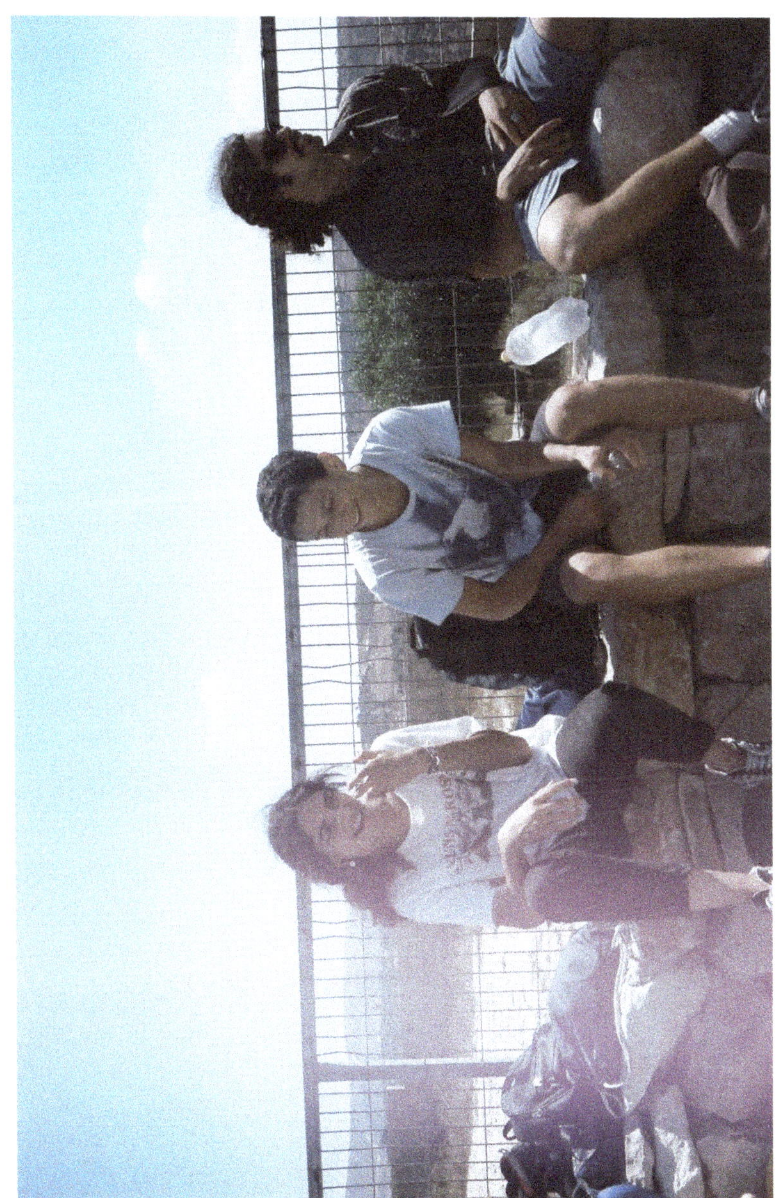

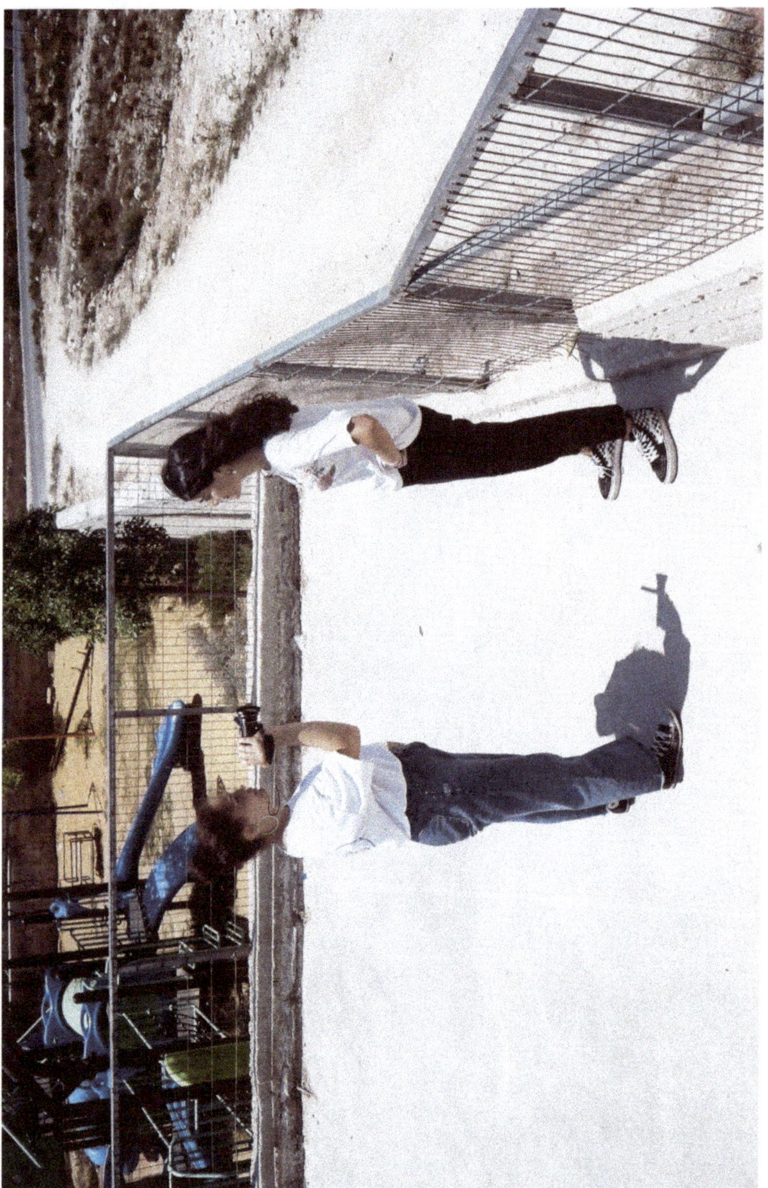

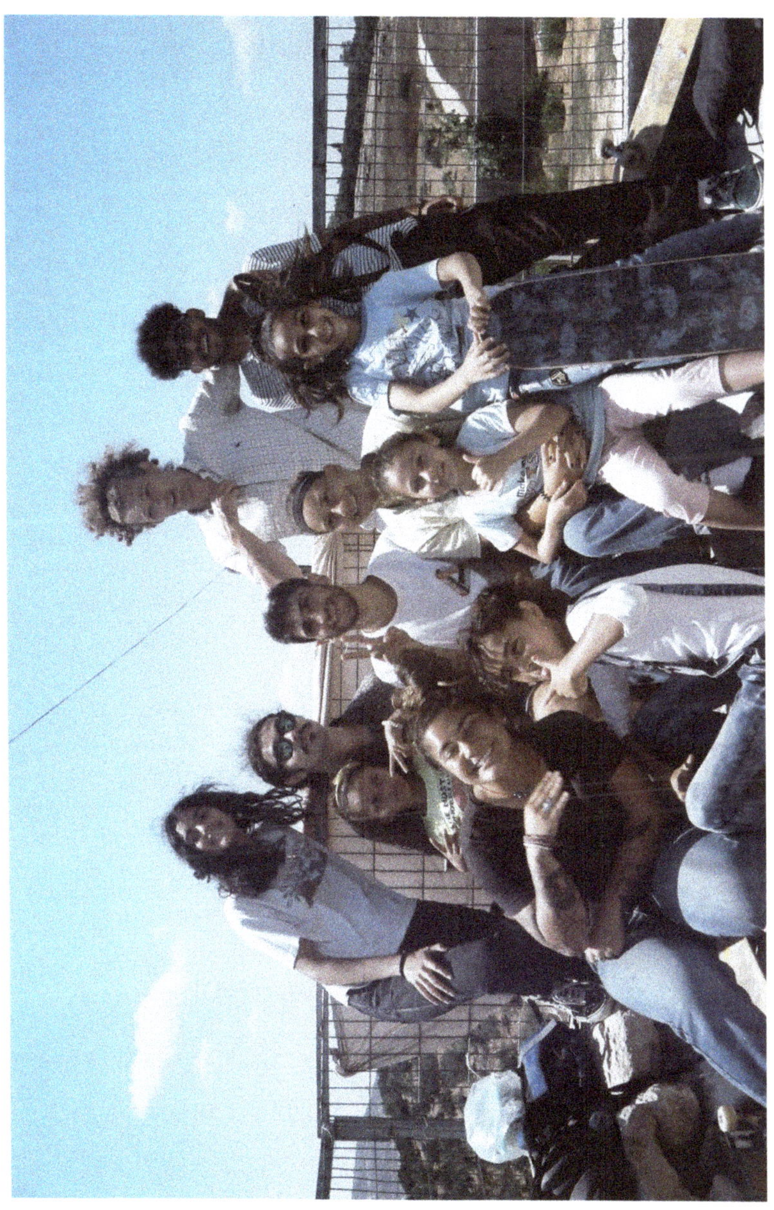

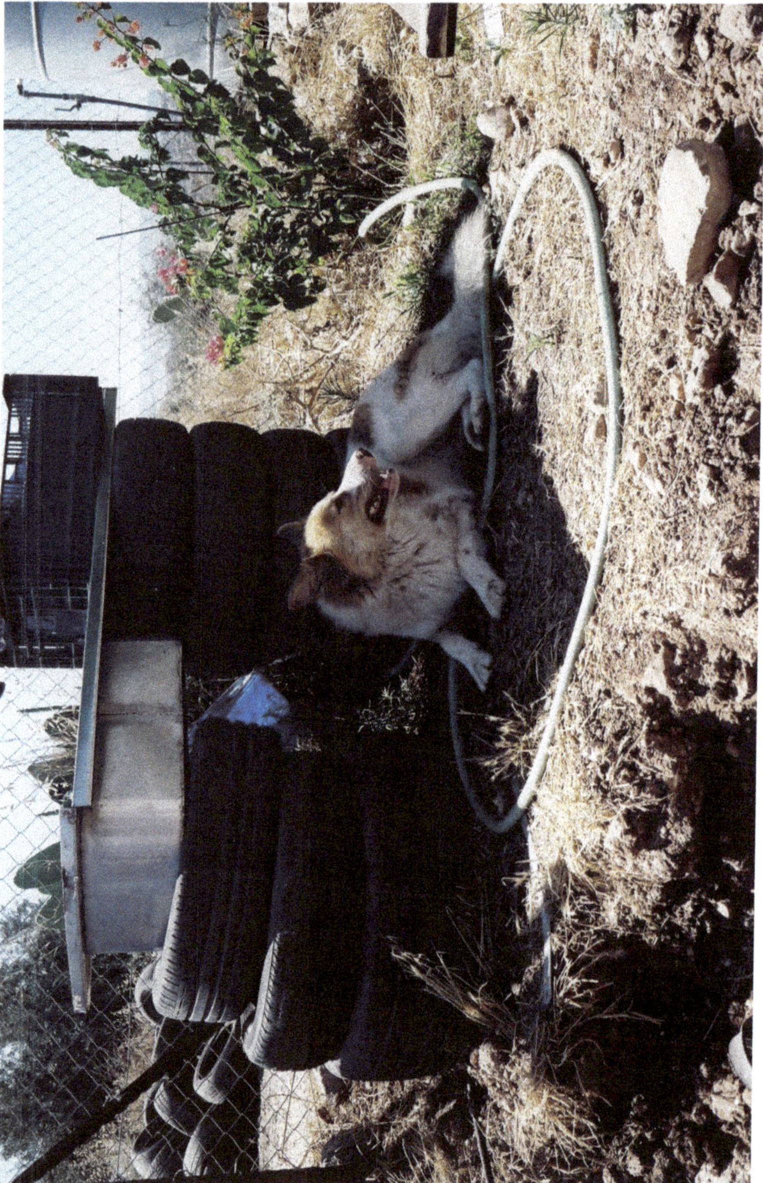

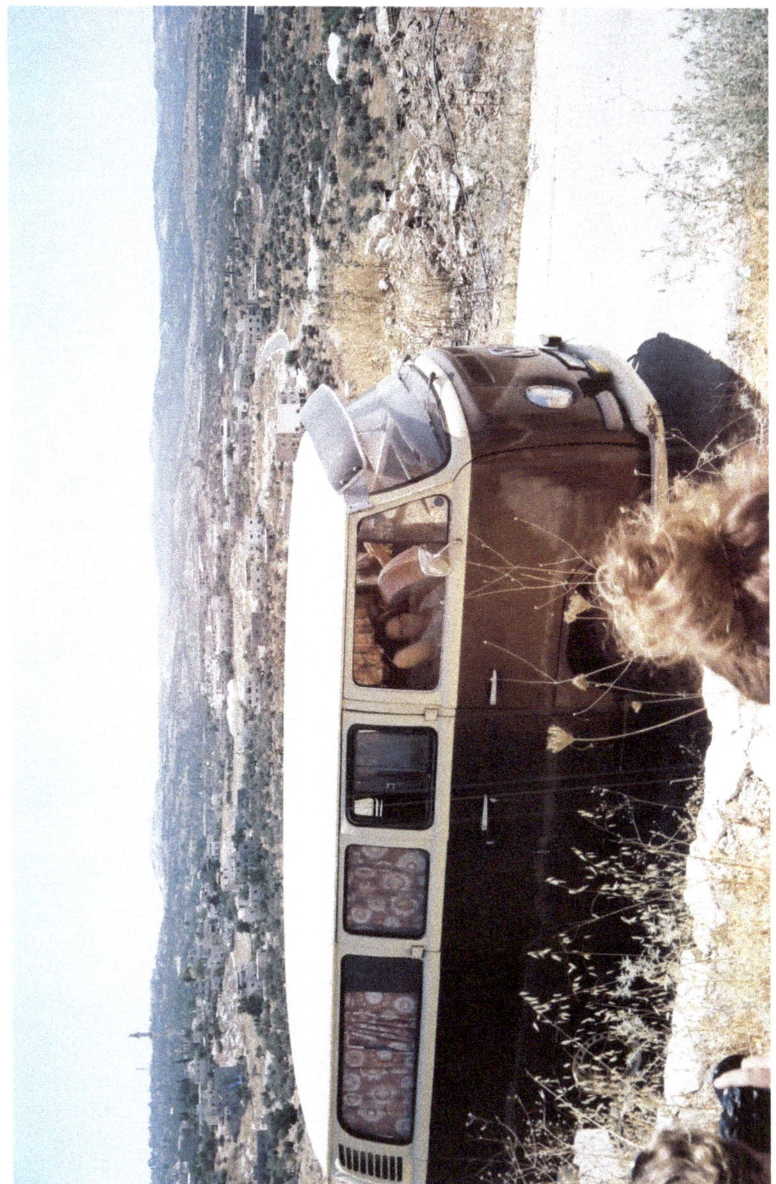

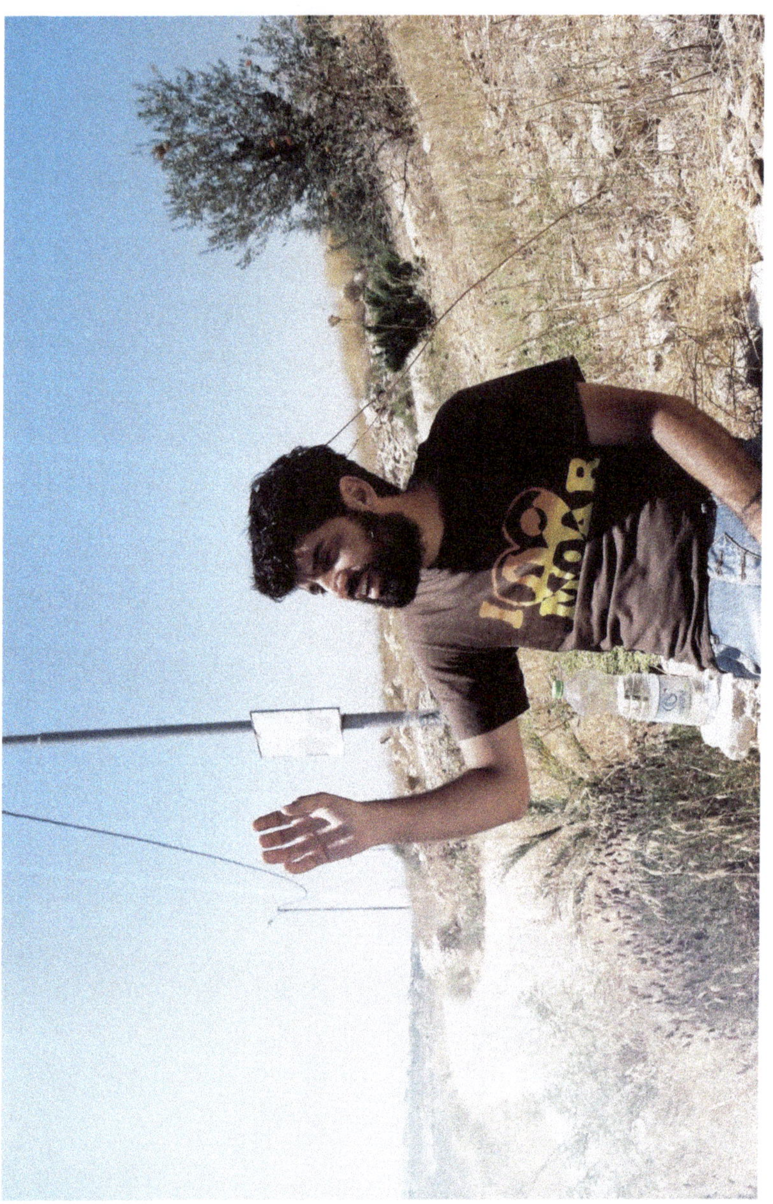

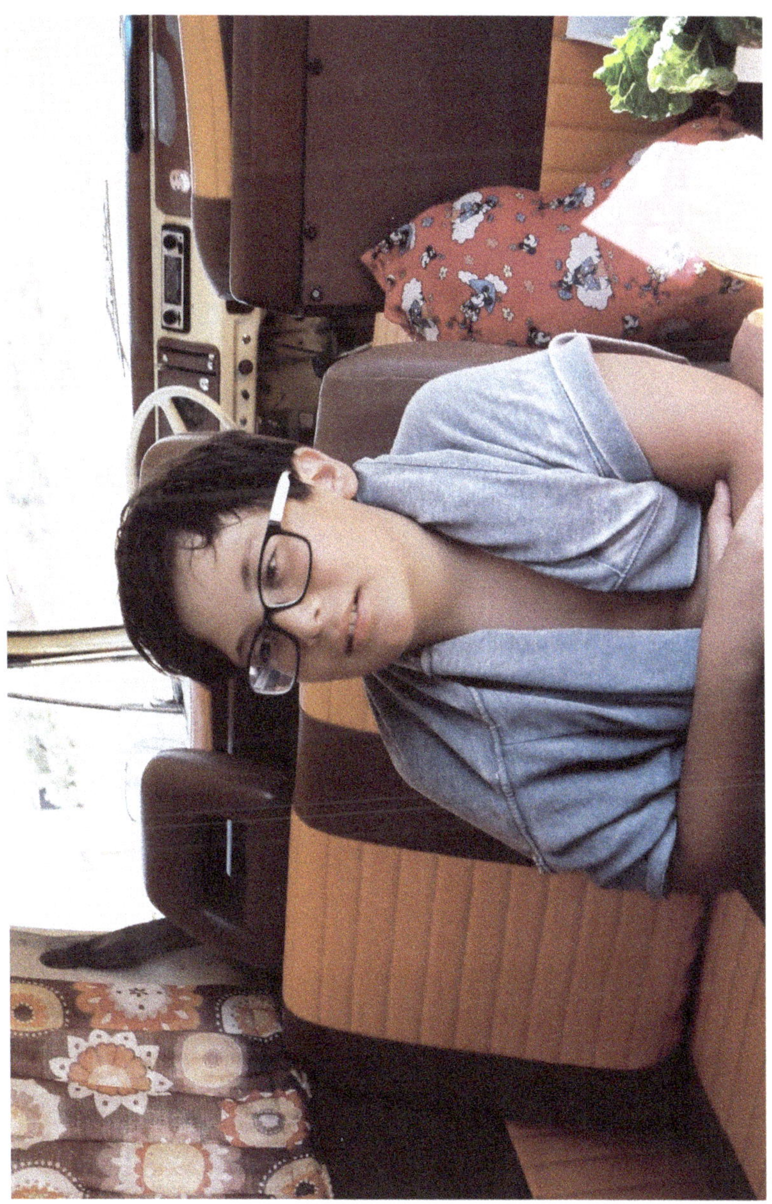

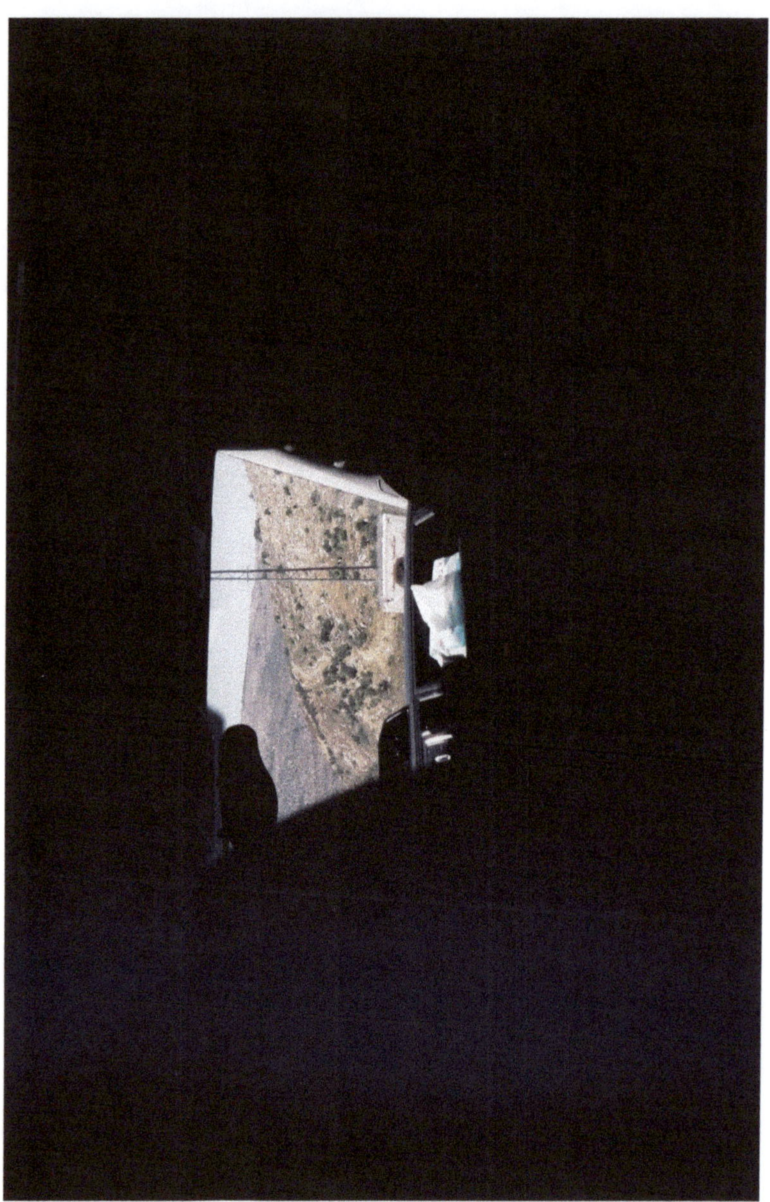

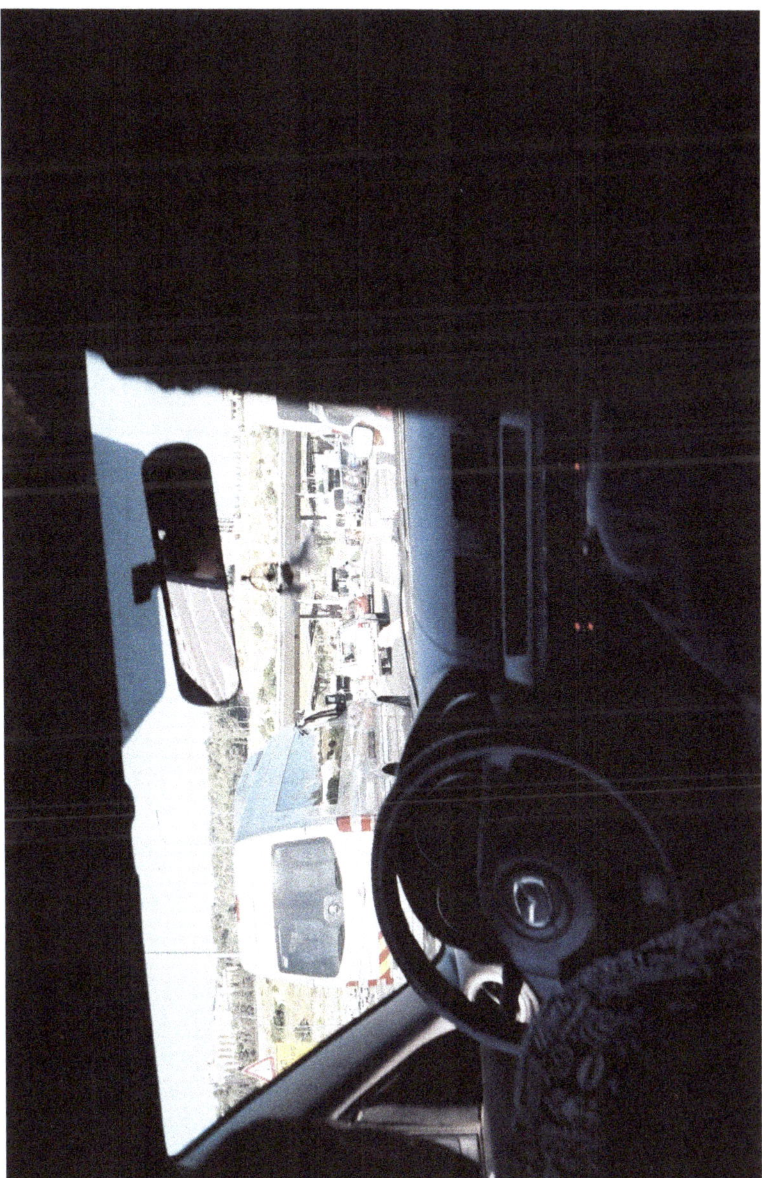

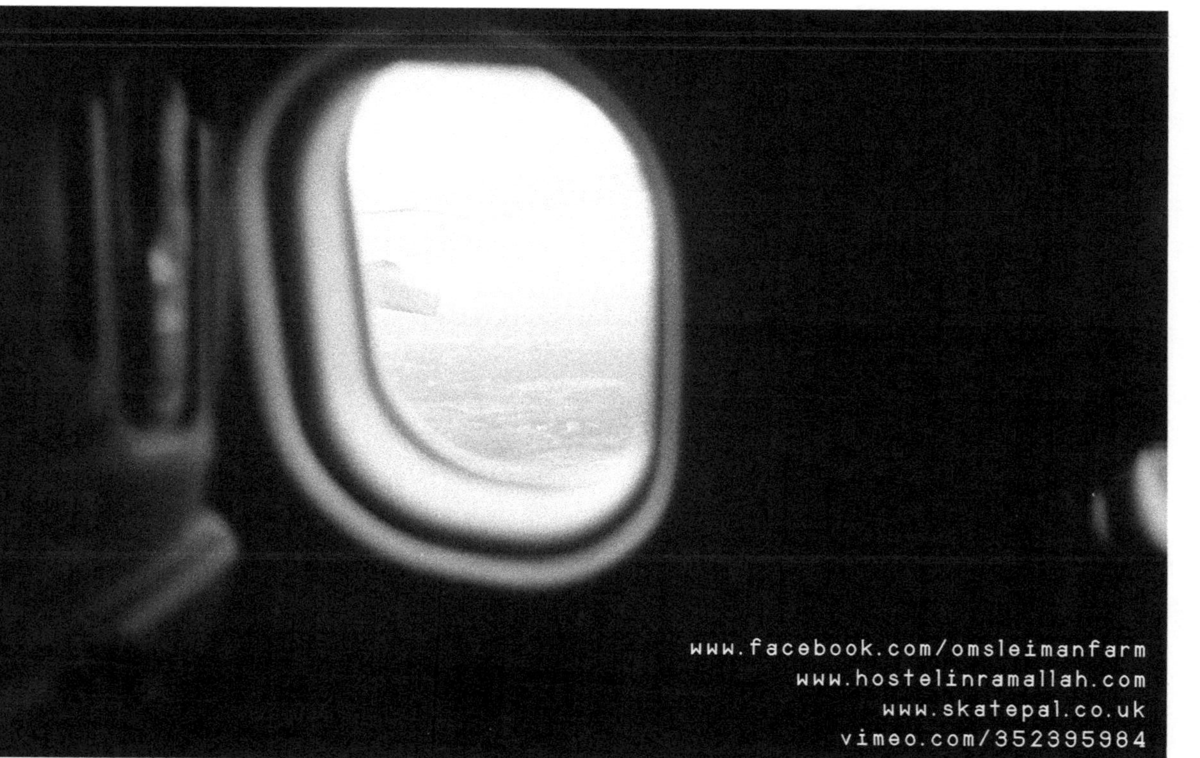

www.barbarianbooks.institute

www.ingramcontent.com/pod-product-compliance
Lightning Source LLC
Chambersburg PA
CBHW050046040726
47599CB00015B/1821